THE HEALING JOURNEY

How a Poor Chinese Village Girl Became an American Healer

The Healing Journey

How a Poor Chinese Village Girl Became an American Healer

Sue Maisano, PhD

Visionary Living, Inc.
New Milford, Connecticut

The Healing Journey:
How a Poor Chinese Village Girl Became an American Healer

By Sue Maisano, PhD

Copyright Sue Maisano, 2018

All rights reserved.
No part of this book may be reproduced in any form or used without permission.

Front cover design by April Slaughter
Back cover and interior design by Leslie McAllister

ISBN: 978-1-942157-23-6 (pbk)
ISBN: 978-1-942157-24-3 (epub)

Published by Visionary Living, Inc.
New Milford, Connecticut
www.visionaryliving.com

Praise for *The Healing Journey* by Sue Maisano:

"*The Healing Journey* by Sue Maisano is an emotionally uplifting story of a poor Chinese girl who defied the odds of who she was expected to become through education and determination. Her story takes you from humble beginnings as a student in rural China to scientist in middle-class America, where her challenges to culturally adapt and find balance within her work and family life helped shape her into the healer she is today. Finding inner power and beauty within her life struggles, her accounts of every day bravery and optimism will inspire and motivate you, while providing lessons for us all. She leaves you wanting to be a better person and feeling more prepared to face life's challenges. This book will truly help awaken your soul!"

– Kimberly Worrell, anthropologist and biologist

"*The Healing Journey* follows the real-life struggles and triumphs of Xu Liu, a poor girl raised in a dirt floor cottage in mainland China, who, through perseverance, courage and optimism, grows up to become Sue Maisano, an American with a doctorate in biology, certified hypnotist, married woman, mother of three, and author of the book you now hold. Throughout her remarkable journey, Sue finds inspiration in the subtle, joy in the darkness, and healing life lessons which are universal to us all. By cultivating gratitude, honoring her dreams, and finding the balance between persistence and acceptance, Sue illustrates how she achieved her unlikely goals, while encouraging her readers to do the same. *The Healing Journey* acts as a reminder that our hardships are our greatest opportunities, our challenges our greatest blessings, and our positive outlook our greatest strength."

– Karin Terebessy, author and yoga instructor

"*The Healing Journey*" by Sue Maisano is an inspiring story of a woman undeterred by the odds. Sue refused to give in to stereotypical expectations of what she was supposed to become. She chose instead to go above and beyond. This is an exhilarating modern "rags to riches" story with a mix of luck and hard work. She details her story of getting out of a poor village in China to raising a successful family in middle class America. It's a new take on the underdog story that we all love to read, where you'll be cheering for Sue to do well and feel the varied emotions and sensations when you read of her numerous rise and falls in her journey to the mountain top. This is a must and highly recommended read for those looking for a thrilling and uplifting story of personal accomplishment against all odds which will awaken their own power within."

– William McCoy, award-winning author, lightworker and successful entrepreneur

Coming to Terms: A Note to the Reader

Throughout *The Healing Journey,* I use the word "Universe" because I believe it is more complete and all-encompassing than alternative terms that are commonly used to define, regardless of your religion or belief systems, the infinite life force and source permeating everything.

I believe "Universe" resonates with a broader audience. However, you can interpret the word by mentally replacing it with anything that makes the most sense in your mind: *God, Buddha, The One, The Source, The Creator, The All Knowing, Higher Intelligence, Divine Intelligence, Spirit, the Infinite*, or whatever else works for you.

As human beings, we still rely on language and words to communicate meaning, but let's look beyond the assembly of letters of the words for now and focus on the true meanings behind them instead, because you will get more out of it when you focus your attention on the true essence of being.

Dedication

*This book is dedicated to men and women
who are searching for the deep meanings of life,
and who choose to awaken to their singular and enormous power
in directing their own lives.*

Author's Note

As Steve Jobs, former CEO of Apple once said:

"You can't connect the dots looking forward; you can only connect them looking backwards. So, you have to trust that the dots will somehow connect in your future. You have to trust in something – your gut, destiny, life, karma, whatever."

Looking back at my life, it was like a storybook to me. Little did I know that I would transform from a poor Chinese village girl feeling helpless and insecure to an American healer whose purpose is to heal and empower others, and an author who's sharing her inspirations and life lessons, as you are reading one of my books right now. In hindsight, the challenges I went through to get where I am today make complete sense. Without them I would not be where I am now.

I wrote *The Healing Journey* not to show off my personal achievements. After all, coming from my humble beginnings, packed with the valuable lessons along the journey I know that I was never alone in life's struggles or accomplishments. Therefore, I don't take full credit for any attainment you might see in this book.

Words can heal and stories empower. This book is written with the intention of awakening the part of you that helps you tap into your true power, which enables you to face any life challenges, difficulties, or frustrations on your journey. My true life stories contained in the following chapters are only the vehicle to convey the empowering message, from a soul being who had walked the path.

Upon reading this book you might see the higher purpose of your life. You might embrace challenges you are currently facing, and therefore deal with it with calmness and confidence. You might see the perfection in your life's journey, no matter where you are right now. You might gain the courage to pick yourself up in life if you fall. You might start seeing "miracles" and "good lucks." You might develop the sense of trust, feeling of destiny, awareness of the higher purpose, and most importantly, the power of your own WILL. My stories are yours, and your stories are mine, because we are interconnected. The human experiences within the stories show us our strength and capabilities as a being.

It is not a coincidence that you are guided to this book, and I am glad that you are ready to take full charge of your life.

Table of Contents

1. Born into Faded Glories — 1
2. From Naiveté to Responsibilities — 25
3. Rewards to My Ambition — 47
4. Passage to America — 63
5. Lessons in Love — 83
6. Finding Mr. Right — 105
7. Balancing Work and Family — 121
8. Finding the Path — 141
9. Lessons in The Higher Purpose — 169

About the Author — 185

Chapter 1

Born into Faded Glories

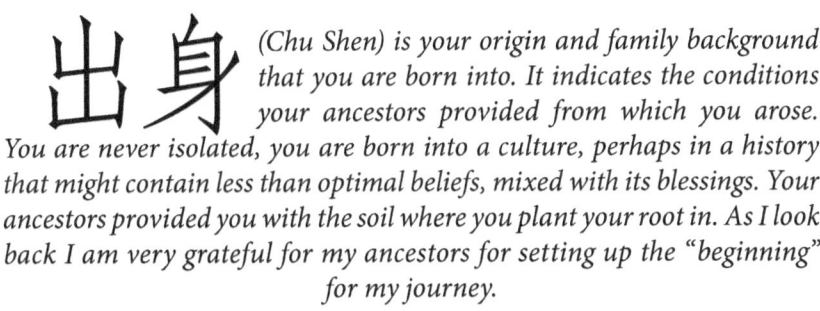 *(Chu Shen) is your origin and family background that you are born into. It indicates the conditions your ancestors provided from which you arose. You are never isolated, you are born into a culture, perhaps in a history that might contain less than optimal beliefs, mixed with its blessings. Your ancestors provided you with the soil where you plant your root in. As I look back I am very grateful for my ancestors for setting up the "beginning" for my journey.*

A Joyful New Arrival

No one comes from nowhere and no one is born into a vacuum.

Your ancestors, their cultural background, and the environment you were born into all have a big influence on you. So, to understand our "beginning" we need to go back further than the day we were born.

My mom's side of the family didn't come from the village where I was born, but from elsewhere.

Her ancestors purportedly had some sort of supernatural powers and were very famous locally for their psychic abilities. My mom's great grandfather was a lawyer, and he built up great wealth and vast land in their native village. However, his young son, my mom's grandfather, in his late teenage years, was a troublemaker; he loved fighting and made some powerful enemies. My mom's great grandfather sensed that the enemies would try to kill them, so to save his family he decided to move to a secret place where nobody knew them.

One night in the early 1920s, the family packed their valuable belongings in a carriage and left their village, abandoning their vast land and houses. My mom's great grandfather found a great spot in Houliyuan Village, in Miyun District, Beijing, and settled down in the village in which I was later born.

The village consisted of about 200 families. Most had been there for generations. The roads inside the village were dirt roads with no names. Places were referenced by the inhabitant's full names or their function, such as the school or the water tower. The houses were tightly packed right next to each other in rows facing the south and people were divided into 12 groups based on the locations of their dwellings. The farmlands were assigned to each family. There was a river flowing through the village, and that's where housewives washed the clothes until the 1990s when the river was drained.

The headquarters of the village was not much different than a resident house, where the important messages were announced through the loudspeaker. Mail and packages to the village were delivered to the headquarters, and your name would be called so you could go and fetch your mail, which was not a frequent event. There was one leader in the village and the relationships among villagers were close, like a family. The best way to describe it is it was like a tribe. Everyone knew one another and they were always able to trace their ancestries to other individuals in the village one way or another. It was a very tight community. Many things there remain the same even today.

My mom's ancestors changed their names to 'Liu' upon settling in Houliyuan Village, one of the most common Chinese surnames, to avoid being tracked by their enemies. No one knew what they were called before, and no one could trace the family back any further than what I have stated here. I learned about my ancestors' stories from my mom, and she learned from her mom and other elders.

The family started anew in Houliyuan Village. They cultivated farms and made a good living in the new village, quickly establishing themselves and purchasing a great deal of land.

My mom's great grandfather became a well-known lawyer locally and everyone sought him out to help with their cases. He would lock himself in his office and imagine the court scenes in his mind and rehearse different roles. He was so eloquent and knowledgeable that he always won his cases. He was building massive wealth for the entire family quickly. However, his son continued to give him headaches.

My mom's grandfather continued to fight, leading groups against the Chinese Communist Party. Unfortunately, his dad was not able to save him this time. The Chinese Communists in the village killed him around 1940 in a mountain range. No one even dared to go and collect his body afterwards. He was only 34 years old when he was killed, and he left behind his wife and three young sons and a daughter. My mom's dad was the second oldest one, and was 11 years old at the time.

My mom's great grandfather supported the entire family, and they lived comfortably on their family wealth. Their properties expanded to almost a third of the village. However, the family glory faded in 1950 when Chairman Mao started the land reform campaign.

During the land reform campaign, rich people's lands, houses, and other properties were taken away from them forcefully by the government and redistributed. People who owned vast land were considered enemies of the country and termed "counter-revolutionaries." Landlords were mistreated and a million of them were executed.

My mom's ancestors went from being glorious to being looked down upon within a couple years, and the vast wealth and properties built from decades of hard work and intelligence suddenly vanished. Not only that, they were humiliated publicly, set as bad examples for people to see, and excluded from many social rights for years to come. Their punishment was harsh.

Being rich and intelligent in that cultural background was a huge detriment and talented people were suppressed and forced to conform to ill-formed rules and regulations. The culture restricted people's talents and punished those who could build wealth through their intelligence and hard work because they were not allowed to be any better than "average."

Sometimes we may look back at history in anger and hatred. How on earth could the government do that to innocent people? We see in retrospect how ridiculous the authorities or long-held wrong ideas might be sometimes. People were mistreated or even slaughtered for no good reason. It might be hard to forgive and let go the emotions.

However, dwelling on the unpleasant past will not get us any further, will not help us progress culturally, socially, and spiritually. People's ideas, mindset, and culture were confined to whatever history they were in, no matter how absurd they look in hindsight. I'm glad that the past has passed. I hope that we all learn from our past mistakes in history and make better decisions now so when we look back in the history of today we don't have any regrets or anger.

My Mom's Childhood

My maternal grandma had long been looked down upon, even by her own mother, simply because she was a woman. When she was born in 1931 she was the third girl in a row. Horribly, her mother was so disappointed that she threw her into the chamber pot right after birth. It was her father who saved her from drowning.

You might think that a mother, being despised as a female growing up herself, would sympathize with her own daughters and treat them well, but that was not the case. On the contrary, oftentimes mothers were the strongest haters of their own daughters in that era in China. If the mother gave birth to a boy, it would somehow elevate her status and reduce her sin, but if she gave birth to a girl it would drag her social status down even further. So, a mother might actually despise her own daughters. The culture was that backwards.

My grandma was never allowed to go to school and never had a single day of education. Her younger sister attended school though, and later became a nurse. She loved the pursuit of knowledge despite her mother's negative intervening. My grandma's younger sister was among the few women who were lucky enough to get an education, solely due to her own ferocious fight for knowledge against her mother's will.

My grandma was fortunate to marry my grandpa, a very smart man who was also believed to have paranormal power. Their parents arranged the marriage, and they had never met each other before their wedding, which was a common practice back then. My grandma was tall and very strong, while her husband was short.

My mom was born in 1960, and was the third surviving child from my grandparents. She has two older brothers and a younger brother.

As I said, it was believed that my mom's father had a type of supernatural power. He could predict the future and was also good at astrology. Nobody knew from whom he learned it or if he got it naturally, but he could read events, and people would come to him for his insight.

When my mom was a young child, she went missing one day and everybody was very concerned about her. But her father did a reading and figured out that she was fine. He predicted where she was, and my grandma was able to follow his instructions to find her. And she was right where he said she'd be.

My grandma was very strict towards the children. She instilled honesty in her children. She could not tolerate the children telling lies or any dishonest behaviors. One time, my mom was sent to fill a bottle of soy sauce at the store. My mom filled it less than full so she could spare some money to buy a candy. This triggered great rage in my grandma when she found out about it, and she beat my mom so bad that my mom couldn't walk for a few days. My grandma was known for being harsh in her methods of educating children and she had extremely high moral standards for them.

Despite the strictness, it was good that my mom received a disciplined upbringing. My grandma regretted in her later years how harsh she had treated her children and how she had not tended to their feelings. When I was in high school visiting my grandma, she told me to be a good girl and be more understanding and considerate so that my mom's life would be better. I sensed that she felt bad for being too harsh with my mom and she wanted to compensate for my mom's bad childhood, and the only way she could do was through me being a good girl to my mom. I understood her feelings of remorse and I knew that she did the best she could from her own limited knowledge in the past.

My mom's favorite brother was two years older than her. He's the one who was beaten the most, as his parents generally vented their anger on him, oftentimes for no reason. He was the smartest child, though. He was able to skip grades in elementary school because he did so well in school. He was also incredibly handsome.

One day, when my mom was about eight years old, her favorite older brother took the pigs out for a walk and my mom went with him. As they passed a big pond, he said, "You wait here for me, Ruzi." (Ruzi was my mom's nickname.) "I'm going into the pond to get some frogs for you." He dove into the pond. My mom, being such a young girl, waited and waited and it took her a long time to realize that her brother had been in the pond for too long. She got worried and screamed for help, but it was too late. When people finally arrived, her brother had long since drowned.

That was a very trying moment for my grandma; she was devastated. Her wonderful son was the smartest of them all, yet he had been treated the worst and was always covered in bruises. Now he was gone without experiencing the good things in life. The guilt and the loss of the innocent, most intelligent child was almost unbearable for my grandma. It took a big toll on her, as she carried the guilt for the rest of her life.

After the loss of the most promising child, my grandparents were left with three children: my mom, and her older and younger brothers. My mom was the only girl in her family, but she wasn't treated any better. My grandpa's frequent bad tempers made my mom's childhood even more difficult. At the time my mom was growing up, girls were still looked down upon in China, and even her father held deep-rooted Chinese beliefs and despised girls.

One time when she was about 13, her dad was so mad at her that he kicked her so hard that she slid across the floor from one room to another. At that age, my mom had long developed the sense of dignity. You can imagine the humiliation she went through, but my mom bit her tongue and didn't say anything. When she was 18, her dad died from tongue cancer. In his later years he lived in agony and pain, and vented towards his wife and children. Ironic justice? We'll never know.

After my grandpa passed away, my grandma eventually remarried. Her new husband had a submissive character and he had never married before, which worked out fine, because he listened to my grandma and devoted his life to the family. Throughout my own childhood and adulthood, he was known as my grandpa, as I never saw my mom's biological dad.

My mom's stepfather was a "non-farmer" and had a secure job from which he could retire. The division between farmers and non-farmers was very strict back then, since only non-farmers could take decent jobs and actually retire with monthly pensions. Plus, their offspring could inherit their job roles. On the other hand, farmers were tied to their farmlands with no retirement or benefits. At the time my grandma remarried, my mom's younger brother was 13 and changed to the stepfather's last name in order to legitimately inherit his job position. The youngest child got the most favor from the stepfather because he would carry on his last name. Also, my mom's younger brother looked just like my mom's older brother who drowned, even though my mom's younger brother was even more attractive. As a result, he was my grandma's favorite because he reminded her of her lost child to whom she owed too much.

Unexpectedly, my mom's younger brother died from a car accident when he was 38 years old, a couple days before he was about to open his shoe company. The tragic event was a huge blow to our family and it was the final straw to my grandma's health. She passed away within a year of my uncle's death while I was in high school.

I heard the stories of my ancestors from my mom and my grandma and it was fascinating to me to see how things had evolved and to bear witness to the family relationships. I loved the stories that I was told, but it was disheartening to hear how the family glory faded. I sympathized with the feelings of women who were despised and the loss of my mom's older brother.

I also deeply understood the feelings that my grandma went through. I liked that my grandpa had some type of inexplicable powers to sense the unknown. I was intrigued by how he did it, but it's forever a mystery for me. I was also very surprised, and immensely grateful that my grandpa put honesty in my soul through kindred spirits, as revealed to me later by my spirit guide. A spirit guide is an advanced being who might have already passed the stage of earthly incarnations, who oversees, teaches, and protects us. It was not until recently that I connected with my spirit guide and was awakened to the possibility of the beyond physical realities, as you will see later in this book.

The fact that my grandpa instilled honesty in my soul tells me that family members who have passed were looking out for us from the higher spiritual plane, even if we didn't perceive their influence with our five earthly senses.

Through my family stories, I got a better understanding of my origin, and I felt blessed to be born into such a family at the right time to carry out my own mission, whatever that turned out to be.

Born into Faded Glories

My Father's Side of the Family

My dad's side of the family has the same family name, "Liu," handed down from generation to generation within Houliyuan Village.

My dad's mom, my paternal grandma, had a poor childhood. She grew up in a small, remote village. Her mom died when she was five years old, and her two-year old sister was so attached to their mom that she cried until she was blind, and died shortly afterwards.

When I heard these stories from my paternal grandma, my heart was broken. Nobody could care for a two-year old who had just lost her mother? A young baby was left in distress and to die? No one would give a helping hand? But as I've talked about, at that social economic and cultural background, losing a baby girl didn't seem to mean much to people. They might have viewed it as one less mouth to feed, especially if it's a girl. They didn't think a girl would amount to anything. The backwards culture was unbelievably sad and disappointing. No one cared for the girls.

My grandma had no education at all. She could recognize her own name in writing, but that was the extent of her reading abilities. As soon as she was old enough, her older sister, who was married to a man in Houliyuan Village, introduced her to my grandpa, my dad's dad.

She soon married my grandpa. When my grandma's older sister died giving birth to her second child, it meant my grandma had no relatives close to her and she then devoted all her life to her growing family. Despite not having any education, she was intuitive and had so many captivating tales from folklore to tell. I was her best listener.

My grandma had six children: three boys and three girls. My dad is her second child and was born in 1958, and he was a very mischievous and humorous character. Since the village was a close-knit community, my dad used to love playing jokes and tricks on people, or simply teasing them and making them laugh.

He and his older brother looked alike, but my dad's older brother was more of a leader, while he was more submissive. My dad would go to the store in the village and buy goodies without paying via credit, but simply signed his brother's name. The store owner would pester my dad's older brother to pay for the goodies as they thought it was my uncle who had actually signed for the goodies. My dad took pleasure in tricking people at a young age.

My dad was very handsome when he was young, but he was overly playful sometimes. He seemed carefree at a young age. He was an elementary school dropout because he hated school and just wanted to play. He would simply go out to play, and when school time was supposed to be over, would come home with his school bag, pretending that he had completed a full day of schooling.

Around the time of third grade, against everyone's advice, and to his eternal regret, my dad dropped out of school. My grandparents were very disappointed by his decision and they did everything they could to "force" him to get an education. Horribly, my grandpa tried to beat school into him, but it didn't work out. His teachers tried to persuade him to go back to school, arguing that he was quite intelligent and would amount to something great one day, but it was in vain. His mind was set on leaving school and he would rather face the consequences. Perhaps he thought he was not right for education, or perhaps he didn't like to be confined to classrooms. Regardless of why, he refused to continue school no matter how much his parents forced him. He was a nature lover, but he seriously lacked discipline.

My dad worked for the village raising cows for the families, and he spent the rest of his childhood that way. His smart brain was wasted, and so, without adequate schooling, no one would hire him for any decent job. He had to take low-paying odd jobs and remained poor for most of his life. He had no one to blame but himself, and the fact that he dropped out of elementary school brought him heartaches throughout his life. If there were a way to go back in time to change his younger self, he would have done it a thousand times.

I now know why he always put such great emphasis on my education when I was growing up. He didn't want me to repeat his mistakes, and he would do anything to support me. He would go from house to house to borrow money for my tuition and never felt any shame in doing so. Throwing away his own opportunity for education was a big life lesson for him, and he learned it the hardest way possible.

Therefore, he knew that he had to make it happen for me to have a brighter future. He would rather face the humiliation of borrowing money from others than missing the opportunity for me to continue education. Looking back, I appreciated his unrelenting support of my studies. Few parents in the village would do that for their children, especially if it were a girl, back then in the culture I was raised. I could not have asked for a better dad.

The Secret Marriage

Even though my dad and mom had known each other from their teenage years in the village, they didn't begin a relationship until they were around 20 years old.

My mom would have loved to have pursued a higher education, but she never had the chance. After her dad died when she was 18, she started working after completing high school. People introduced potential boyfriends to her but, despite some eligible candidates, my mom's heart was set on the most mischievous one, the one who happened to work at the same factory in the village at the time.

My mom's mom was strongly against their relationship. She didn't like my dad's background, and hoped her daughter would marry someone from a better family who had some money and an education, so she would live an easier life.

But my dad was a pleasant person. He was honest, trustworthy and humorous, despite the mischief. Perhaps that's why my mom fell in love with him.

One day, my dad helped my mom and her family plant sweet potatoes in their farm. Afterwards, they secretly went and acquired a marriage certificate. My mom didn't tell anyone, not even her own mom. That was May 17, 1981, but they weren't able to live together because their marriage wasn't official yet; it was still a secret.

When my mom's mom found out, she was mad as hell. She scolded my mom and said she would not recognize her as her daughter, and would expel her from the family. But my mom stood by her decision; there was a strong attraction force binding my parents together, and this would not be denied.

After they got married, my mom and dad still were not able to live together. They were able to consummate their marriage on November 1, 1981, however, and soon after that, my mom learned that she was pregnant with me.

When my dad's family found out, they wanted to arrange a proper wedding. My dad's family went to talk to my mom's uncles and had them talk to my grandma. Having my mom pregnant and not officially married would mean people would think my mom was loose and it could ruin her reputation, so despite the fact that my grandma wasn't thrilled, she had no other choice but to acquiesce. In addition, she wanted the upcoming baby, me, to have a whole family with the real dad.

Perhaps it was partly due to my mom's poor childhood that my grandma really wanted my mom to have a happy and rich life herself. My dad's family certainly wasn't the nice family my grandma had hoped for and envisioned for her daughter. She also didn't like my dad's mischievous behaviors and how he didn't seem to take anything seriously. She didn't want my mom to regret her marriage later on. But she saw that there was nothing she could do to stop my mom from carrying out her wishes, and not agreeing with her choice would only do her harm. She reluctantly blessed the marriage and wished the new couple a good life.

The Rising Sun

My parents celebrated their wedding when my mom was already five months pregnant with me. Afterwards, they lived with my dad's entire family. By that time, my dad's older brother was also married, but his other four siblings were still young. With so many people sharing the same house it was very crowded.

Later during the pregnancy, the family decided that it was no longer possible for everyone to live together. It was agreed that the married members, my dad and his older brother, should move out with their wives and build their own houses.

My dad's older brother was a very able man, very strong, and with good people skills. He moved out first, finding a nearby spot to build their house.

My mom and dad remained with the extended family a while longer. They were very frugal and extremely poor. Even though my mom was pregnant, she didn't have the privilege of eating more nutritious food than anyone else and she barely had enough to eat in general.

Thankfully, though, she had a smooth pregnancy, and on August 13, 1982, I was brought into the world at 4:15 pm. A midwife from our village facilitated the delivery and I was born at home. I weighed five pounds and was tiny, but also very hairy. My mom thought that I looked like a mouse!

My mom was concerned because I looked so tiny. She felt bad because she couldn't afford the nutrition that I needed. There was a sense of guilt from day one, but I know that she did the best she could.

Despite my size, I was a healthy and strong baby. My parents named me Xu (旭), which means "the rising sun at 9 o'clock." It symbolizes radiating light and energy. My parents hoped that I would turn into an aspirational person.

When I was a few months old, my parents decided that we should move out because it wasn't possible to get the necessary food and care living with such a big family. But they didn't have any money to build their own house from scratch. My dad talked to his older brother and he kindly agreed to let my dad buy his house while he would build a new one next to ours, and it all worked out well.

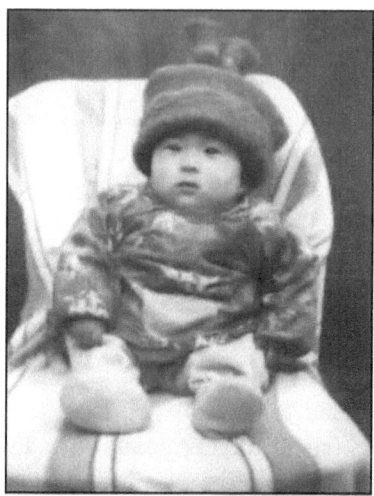

This is the first photo taken of me, at only 100 days old. Note the hands behind the chair giving me support.

After our new house had been built, it was very raw looking. In this part of the country our houses were built with bricks and cement. The floor was dirt unless you put down cement or tile. My parents had no money to do any work on the house when they moved in.

Heat was generated from a small coal stove that also served as the cooking and water-boiling stove. The stove was connected to a metal tube as the chimney to vent the gas out of the room through the window. One would have to be careful about carbon monoxide poisoning. Gas poisoning was a common accident in northern China back then due to the bad practices and lack of gas detection. Unless you planted yourself right next to the stove, the house was very cold in the winter. My mom said that when we first moved in it was wintertime and I was just a few months old. I cried inconsolably from the cold and my tears froze into ice.

Even though I don't have memories of the harsh environment that I was living in, I could imagine the poor baby crying in the cold and the young parents feeling helpless that they couldn't afford anything better. That was our life back then.

My parents couldn't afford vegetables; dinner would be cooked rice with salt. Despite the lack of nutrition, I was a very healthy and active baby, and I loved to see new things. My favorite sight was looking at green leaves. Whoever was holding me had to carry me from place to place to see new spots with green leaves. I was very demanding for new things and staying in one spot or staring at one place never worked! My mom told me that I was a difficult baby in that regard because I made the caretaker's job difficult. When I became a teenager, I heard relatives saying I was very alert and active as a baby, and it was a difficult task to babysit me.

Perhaps the green leaves had a calming effect on the baby me and gave me a sense of growth and hope. It provided me a means to look beyond the harsh environment I was living in and gave me a feeling of peace and vitality. It's striking how little has changed. I still love seeing green leaves and they inspire me.

My mom's mom helped take care of me, even though she still didn't get along with my dad. In fact, my dad told me one time he visited my grandma and her family while she was loudly badmouthing my dad. When she saw my dad walk in, she immediately went silent and it was very awkward. My dad carried this with him, telling me the story many times, and clearly there was friction between him and my grandma for many years.

In retrospect, I know that deep down my grandma wasn't really against my dad. She was concerned about her daughter and wanted a well-established man for her daughter so that she could live a much better life, a respite from the hardships from childhood. It was my grandma who carried the guilt of treating my mom harshly when she was a child and she wanted compensation for my mom. My dad on the other hand was the best man my mom could have married. He was very caring and tended to my mom's needs. He treated my mom's family as his own throughout the years and my grandma witnessed how great my dad treated my mom and their entire family. It took them nearly 10 years to truly understand and accept each other and reach a real harmonious stage in the relationship.

Sometimes we need to step into other people's shoes and really understand and appreciate them. You may find that the other person isn't really that different than yourself. In fact, you might have the same good intention, the only difference could be you are viewing things through different perspectives. The more you let go of your expectations of others the more you can embrace other people's natural qualities.

THE ONE CHILD POLICY: NOT IN MY FAMILY

My dad's older brother and his wife had a girl too, one year before I was born. At that time, China had a strict one-child policy. Any couple known to have given birth to a second child was fined 1,680 Yuan. Bear in mind that, back then, the average monthly income was less than 50 Yuan!

My uncle and his wife took the chance. They had their second child and it was a boy. My uncle was so excited that he happily paid the fine, because a boy would carry on the family name. Girls were considered like water, something you pour out and never get anything back from.

My mom saw how excited my uncle was, and imagined how happy my dad would be if she could give him a boy, too. She broached the subject, but my dad said, "A girl is good enough. And life will be easier with just one child."

He didn't care about carrying on the family name; he just loved my mom and me. In addition, my dad didn't want to face the financial burden. However, even though my dad said a daughter was fine, my mom wanted to make my dad happier. My mom didn't have apparent prejudice against girls, but she still thought having a boy would make it complete.

So, she went to see her mom's younger sister, who was a nurse. Her aunt took out her IUD secretly, and my mom eventually conceived another child. Somehow my mom knew it was a boy. She lied to the local government and said that the IUD failed to work. She argued for a 50 percent discount on the fine, they granted the accommodation, and my brother ended up costing 800 Yuan. My parents got their baby boy three and a half years after I was born. My parents were both thrilled. My mom's wish was fulfilled.

It was ridiculous that the government restricted people's family planning in China and it was particularly strict in the 1980s and 1990s. Couples that conceived a second child were punished financially by a hefty fine and through other means, including getting fired from their jobs. The one child policy, compounded with the prejudice against girls, resulted in many girls as the first child being abandoned so the parents could have a second "chance" for a boy. The problem was particularly serious in the remote villages where people's awareness and education were almost nonexistent.

While my mom was pregnant with my brother, at the age of 26, she was working at a local brick factory. She didn't want people to know that she was pregnant and luckily her belly wasn't too pronounced until much later.

It was heavy work, making bricks from raw materials. Every day my mom would go to work with me, and the goat we had. The goat was pregnant too. She would put the goat in a field to eat grass and I would play in the factory. I had lots of fun.

My mom had much better nutrition when pregnant with my brother since they lived independently from the big family. When my brother was born he was much bigger, and weighed almost eight pounds. His skin was brighter, and he was much less hairy than I was. He was beautiful, and perfect in my parents' eyes. My parents were very excited to have their baby boy and they named him Kai (凯), which means, "Come back with victory."

As soon as I was self-aware, I confronted my mom and asked her if she liked my brother more than me. Would she have considered having a second child if I had turned out to be a boy? She said she loved us equally. She told me the reason she wanted a second child was because

This is me at two years old. I was so intimidated at the photographer's studio in town that I held onto my mommy instead of posing by myself.

she didn't want me to be the only child supporting my parents in their old ages. It seemed to make sense, but I still believed that if I were a boy my mom would not have wanted a second child. I do love my brother and could not imagine a life without him. But I could feel that my mom always treated him as her pride and joy, even though she didn't dislike me in any way. My mom put her real hope in my brother, and I always knew that. It manifested as harsh punishments to me whenever I didn't take good care of my younger brother. My dad sided with me more often than my mom when I was growing up.

Neither of my parents was as bad as many other parents I knew whose only concerns were their sons. I knew of many stories in which parents persuaded their daughters to drop out of school or give up their dreams and start working to support the male offspring. Whenever that happened, my parents were awed at how stupid the parents were in sacrificing their daughters for their sons. They hated that type of behavior and would never do that to me. In that regard, my parents were wise and gave me enough room to grow and provided me with equal opportunity. Therefore, I never felt lesser than my brother. I was aware of my mom liking my brother more, but it didn't bother me much.

Each gender has its own unique traits, and as spiritual beings with a human body each one of us have been males and females through multiple lifetimes. There is no point in prejudice against one gender or the other as both are equally indispensable for the advancement of the human race and society. Fortunately, advancement in people's awareness as well as cultural changes is taking place right now in China, and girls are being valued more and more.

A Fateful Dream

My parents had high hopes for my brother. They believed that their lives would change forever after he was born. And life did change, but in the wrong direction! The joy of a new addition to the family did not last long.

All dressed up at three years old in my new dress and hat. I was nervous sitting on the rocking horse inside the photographer's studio.

When my brother was less than a month old, my mom had a vivid dream one night. Three beings came to talk to her. One of them she identified as her father, who had passed away when she was 18. She couldn't identify the other two beings. They said they had come to warn my mom, because the life in front of her was too good for her destiny. They told her that she needed to be tested to show that she deserved a good life. She was going to endure ordeals and experience extreme pains and difficulties in the next 10 years to test her abilities.

In the dream my mom was worried and said she needed to take care of her new baby and that she couldn't die. The intelligent beings reassured her that she wasn't going to die, but it was going to feel like her skin was being ripped off.

They then offered a solution to avoid all the suffering and told her to listen carefully and to do everything they said. The being she identified as her father said, "I need you to prick your middle finger and let it bleed onto a carrot. That way you will avoid the ordeals that are about to happen to you." And the being asked her, "Do you remember now?" My mom said, "Yes." He repeated, "Do you remember now?" And my mom said, "Yes." He repeated it a third time: "Do you remember now?" My mom said, "Yes!" And then the beings disappeared, and my mom awoke immediately in terror.

The nightmare was crystal clear and felt so real. As the clock hit midnight she heard our neighbor's dog chasing down the street, barking furiously. She sensed that that was probably the intelligent beings going away. She was awed by the dream but very frightened by the message.

The next day she talked to her mom, who told her that it was just a dream, and cautioned her that she shouldn't take it too seriously. My mom let it go and didn't follow the instructions given to her in the dream. But, soon after, she was struck by a strange illness. She couldn't keep anything down; she threw up everything and she had extreme abdominal pains. It felt like her internal organs were being twisted and crushed. According to ancient Chinese texts, carrots in dreams denote prosperity and health. Unfortunately, neither my grandma nor my mom knew of it or thought in that direction.

Born into Faded Glories

When a photographer came to the village, our uncle and aunt next door paid for this photo of me, five years old, and my brother Kai (凯), two years old. Notice the pile of corn stacked up on the windowsill.

My brother was still a newborn when my mom was hospitalized. My grandma, my dad's mom, took care of my brother while I was taken to my mom's mom.

Strangely enough, the hospital couldn't detect what was wrong with my mom. Every test showed that she was completely normal, yet the severe pain continued. She was transferred to one of the best hospitals in Beijing. My dad stayed at my mom's bedside all the time, taking care of her. As a result, he was not able to work.

This continued for several months, and still there was no diagnosis. It seemed that she was dying, and no one could pinpoint the cause. In the same hospital that my mom was in, another patient, a young man, had similar symptoms. He ultimately couldn't stand the pain anymore and jumped off the hospital roof to his death.

My mom felt useless, as if some force possessed her. Life didn't seem to be worth living and she just wanted to end the suffering. One day, she too jumped from a third-floor window of the hospital. Fortunately, there was a tree beneath the window, which she hit on the way down to the ground. The tree saved her life; but her bones were broken throughout her body and she was seriously injured.

After the accident, one of my mom's cousins went to inform my grandma, my dad's mom, of what had happened. He was in such a terrible emotional state, however, that he chose the wrong words to tell the story. My grandma was so shocked, because she now believed that her daughter-in-law had jumped to her death. She collapsed and dropped my baby brother onto the cement floor.

This accident, combined with the fact that he had been forced to eat solid food before his stomach was developed enough for it due to lack of money to buy formula, resulted in my brother having a very tough start in life.

After my mom's fractures healed, my parents returned home, as it was clear the hospital couldn't help any more. Doctors had given up on her and some had suggested non-traditional treatments.

My mom continued to suffer pain for the following 10 years and no doctor could tell what was wrong with her. However, when she was around 36 years old, the strange pain subsided on its own. We accumulated a lot of debt because of the multitude of hospital bills and the fact that my dad couldn't find any decent jobs. He worked at construction jobs, clothing factories, and welding. But his main focus had always been taking care of my mom.

Looking back at my mom's fateful dream, I now believe it could have been a message from the higher spiritual plane. The entity she recognized as her dad in her dream came to warn her of an upcoming health issue and told her how to avoid it. In her dream, her dad's spirit confirmed with her three times to make sure that she indeed understood and would carry out the action mentioned. She also had the inner knowing in the dream, and upon awakening, that it was something serious and meaningful. However, she didn't follow her intuition and take action.

Sometimes the messages we receive seem bizarre and incomprehensible, and therefore we doubt our intuition and brush it aside. But it takes trusting the Universe and staying in tune with our true selves to become receptive to messages coming from the higher spiritual plane.

On the other hand, my mom being affected by a strange illness that could not be detected by medical instruments and caused suffering for 10 years may have a deeper meaning for the greater good. What good could stem from it? Could it be arranged before reincarnation? Was there a lesson for everyone involved from which to learn and grow? I believe so.

My mom was tested for her strength and courage to live on. My dad's love for my mom was tested. Because of the condition she was in, it challenged me to become very independent early on around the age of 10. I witnessed what suffering was and it cultivated a burning desire in me to help people relieve pain and sufferings. My brother became resilient to stress since he was a baby and he developed a sense of humor to laugh at difficult times instead of being crushed by it. In retrospect, my mom's fateful dream and her strange illness was a blessing in disguise.

Chapter 2

From Naiveté to Responsibilities

懂事 *(Dong Shi) describes a child growing up and starting to become sensible, thoughtful, intelligent, and understands what is going on. This chapter is the story of how I realized at a very early age that there was only one way for me to escape the cycle of poverty into which I was born, and to begin to rewrite what was supposed to be my fate.*

Stubborn Girl Never Got What She Wanted

I was a very rebellious and stubborn girl growing up. When I was 7 years old, one time my mom cut my hair short, like a boy, and I yelled, "I don't like this hair, grow my hair back." First my mom was amused and said, "How can I grow your hair back?" But, seeing her amused and smiling, I knew I was safe to go mad. I yelled even louder, "Grow my hair back!" My mom became serious and her face got very stern. She said, "You're making no sense. You need to stop crying and behave." But I refused. As I said, I was a very stubborn kid. I threatened, "If you don't grow my hair back, I'm going to leave and never come back." My mom didn't buy into that and said coldly, "So go. I don't care."

I couldn't believe how horrible my mom was. She didn't even try to stop me from leaving. I was expecting her to at least beg me to stay, or to say something nice so that I could forgive her with dignity. But she didn't. I started running out of the house, expecting her to chase after me. But she didn't.

When I reached the gate of our house, I was afraid to run any further. It was nighttime, and I was terribly afraid of the dark. I was hoping my mom would come and get me, so I could go home. But she didn't! I stayed at the gate for a long while, waiting for her to show up, but it never happened. In the end, I wandered back to the house by myself, and there was no apology from my mom. I felt so embarrassed. I began to doubt that she was even my real mom. After all, no real mom would allow her daughter to run away, right?

I then threatened to starve myself to death. I felt sure my mom would give in and apologize to me. That's all I wanted. But she didn't.

I was in first grade at the time. I didn't eat dinner that night, nor breakfast the next day. When it was around lunchtime at school I was so hungry, I almost started to hallucinate. I also got incredibly sleepy. Eventually, I couldn't keep my mind on my studies, and I raised my hand and told my teacher that I was very hungry. My teacher laughed and asked, "Why are you so hungry?" I said, "I got into a fight with my mom and I decided not to eat anymore. And now I'm really hungry." My teacher gave me permission to go home early for lunch. Later, she told another teacher how cute I was for raising my hand in class and telling her about my hunger. I went home and ate an early lunch, but my mom acted as if nothing had happened.

She never gave in to me. It was a hard lesson to learn, that I could never threaten my mom to get what I wanted. She taught me that I had to give in sometimes. She never bought into my nonsense or my tantrums.

From Naiveté to Responsibilities

Growing up, I was very obstinate, and it was frustrating to not get what I wanted. I would try all my tricks on my mom. By what seemed like my mom heartlessly not responding to my requests, I was forced to learn to curb my desires. I also learned to never use others' weaknesses to get what I want for selfish reasons. Looking back, I'm glad that she didn't spoil me in any way at all. Instead she disciplined me and, even though I didn't like it at the time, I appreciate the moral standards she instilled in me at such a young age.

Stories Instead of Books

Growing up, I didn't have any books to read. Instead I loved to listen to stories, especially those from my dad's mother. She always had a tale to tell, stories she picked up from older people she had known when she herself was growing up as a young girl. I had been listening to her stories as far back as I could remember. The way my grandma told the stories was always captivating, and the simple stories tell big life lessons and teach you to be a good person.

I especially loved the stories of a paranormal or supernatural nature, and even ghost stories. I was intrigued by stories about such subjects and wondered if they were real. When it came time to sleep, I would get scared thinking about the stories I had just heard, but I would still beg my grandma for more stories the next day.

As a young girl growing up in rural China I often wondered why I was here on this earth. I thought I was always going to be a child to eternity and my parents, grandparents, and anyone else I knew were going to stay the way they were, until I was old enough to realize that life is like the flowing water and we were all growing towards older age. This meant to the younger me that one day my grandma would perish.

I was very sad to realize this. Why was I born in the first place if I were to be gone one day? Would I be so sad that I didn't even want to continue my own life when my grandma died? Would life still be meaningful once the people I knew growing up were all gone? I had so many curiosities, and they made me very sentimental.

I was intrigued by these seemingly big questions that were beyond my comprehension. My grandma reassured me, though, that she would be still watching me from the other side once she moved on. She said I was too silly to feel sad because things would evolve, and I would make new connections in the world. I felt the sense of "flow" and "change," even though I was not able to understand the deep meanings of life.

I was born with a big mole right in the middle of the back of my neck. According to Chinese culture and beliefs, a mole on the back means that you'll have a hard life of struggle and heavy work.

My grandma was long concerned about me. She certainly didn't want my life to turn out to be hard, with heavy labor. She consulted some elders and was told, instead, that a mole on the back of the neck meant that I would always have important people helping me at critical times in my life. Apparently, rather than an indication of a hard life, it was a sign of good fortune.

She was satisfied and relieved with the answer, and then told me. I know it's probably superstition but, looking back, I have received unexpected help from important people in times of need. You will see later in my story that perhaps my grandma was right.

Sibling Rivalry

As a teenager, my brother and I got on very well. We were good friends, but we were also rivals. It was a healthy sibling type of rivalry, however. Sometimes Kai liked to challenge me and, while I was very humble, he was the opposite. He would brag about how smart he was and tried to bring me down by comparison, not with any evil intent, but as a challenge to his big sister.

Kai was a very active and strong boy. I was his big sister. He always wanted to wrestle with me and prove who was stronger before he would start listening to me.

When I was around 12 and Kai was 9, we were in a wheat field and locked in an argument. He said, "I'll listen to you only if you can beat me in a fight." At that point, he was getting very big and strong, so I was a little intimidated. I was scared that if I lost the fight, he would use it to humiliate me. But, at the same time, I still wanted him to show respect to his big sister and listen to me.

Driven by adrenalin I guess, I jumped into a fight with him. After a few rounds, I captured him on the ground. It was such a victory, but it was the last time I can remember beating him. As he grew bigger and stronger I avoided getting into physical fights with him.

Kai was a bright student in elementary school, but his scores were as unpredictable as the stock market. In one school year, he earned the full score for every course, and in the next year, he would fail them all. The teachers liked and disliked him at the same time.

He had a smart mind, but lacked discipline – everything depended on his mood. He still acted very proud of himself, bragging that he could pass exams even without putting much effort in, a self-aggrandizing stance taken by most of the elementary school boys in town back then.

My mom forced him to study and devoted 90 percent of her attention to him. Because of this constant supervision, my brother developed resistance and was not very fond of my mom. He would complain to me that she was too strict with him. But looking back, without this attention, guidance, and sometimes punishment, who knows if he would have developed into the good person he became?

Since my brother began disobeying my mom because of her tight supervision, I was assigned to look after him, since he somewhat respected me. I was always very concerned with my little brother growing up and I helped him as much I could. It wasn't because he was the male offspring of the family, but because I saw great good, and great potential in him. He needed a lot of discipline to stay on track, overcome his shortcomings, and use his talents. Seeing me doing well in school would encourage him.

I was the one who was very easy to deal with, and I needed no motivation to study or do housework. After school during my elementary school years, I would study on the dresser. I would stand there and read textbooks or do my homework. My brother always laughed at me and said, "You study so hard, but look at you! You're not a top student! That means you're stupid!" I simply smiled, as I knew he was teasing me. But one time I couldn't put up with him anymore and replied, "A smart student studies hard because a smart student understands that it requires effort. And knowing that you need to put in effort is part of the intelligence." That silenced him for a while.

Growing up with my brother Kai was challenging and he always pushed me to become a better person. I always wanted to set a good example for him because that would be the best way for him to learn and trust. Our traits complement each other. I was diligent and humble; he was clever and humorous. But we also had a lot in common. We were both compassionate, honest and righteous. Sometimes we secretly admire each other, but we also challenge each other to see things from a different perspective. It is a blessing to have such a brother.

My Dad's Piglet

My dad loved nature. His love of animals was contagious and spread to my brother and me. When I was about 8 years old, our next-door neighbor's pig gave birth to 10 piglets, the last of which was so tiny and frail that they decided to give him up. My dad heard about this, took him home, and raised him.

He was very caring to animals and he treated his little piglet very well. He put a bowl of food out for him, but would draw a circle on the ground and move his hands three times around the circle. The piglet followed my dad's gesture and made three circles around the bowl before he was allowed to eat.

He was a very intelligent pig with my dad's training and, because my dad combed his hair to increase his blood circulation, he grew up bigger and stronger than all his siblings next door. The way my dad raised animals made me feel that animals were just like humans and I was intensely emotionally involved with each animal we raised.

Unfortunately, a Chinese holiday drew near, and my mom decided to have the pig killed so that we could sell the meat for money. I went with my dad to the butcher's, but I couldn't watch it. I ran as far as I could to avoid the pig's cry, but it was impossible. I still heard it and was heartbroken.

My family sold the meat on the village street and we had enough left over for ourselves. But neither my brother nor I could eat any. We were simply too sad.

What Little Brown Taught Me

We also raised other animals from time to time, but it always took a heavy toll on my brother and me in the end. The problem was we fell in love with our farm animals.

When I was 12 years old, my dad bought a white goat that was pregnant. She was a very picky eater, and my brother and I were both worried about her baby. But the kid was born big and healthy, and we called him "Little Brown" because he was brown while the mother was pure white. We heard that the father was also white, so we were not sure why Little Brown turned out to be so special, but we loved him dearly.

Little Brown was a good eater and he loved to play with us. Sometimes I would hold out my fist and he would come close and put his head against it. I would push on his head and he would push back with all his strength. We were wrestling with each other. He looked so serious and wanted to win so badly, just like my little brother!

He was such a pleasant addition to our early teenage life. Sometimes we would be eating, and he would walk up to us, put his front legs up and hold onto me. He nodded his head and used the gesture to tell me to lower my hand with food so he could reach it. I would first tease him and raise my hand before I would lower it for him.

Little Brown was like a human to my brother and me. In fact, he was much superior to many of the people we knew, because his eyes were so innocent and full of wonder.

My mom soon decided to have him spayed, meaning that he would never have babies. This made me sad, as though his right to father a child had been violated.

Part of my job on the farm was to take the goats out to eat grass after school. It was so quiet that my mind used to wander while the goats ate peacefully. I thought about a folk tale I had heard about a young man who went to fetch wood in the mountains. While in the mountains, he saw two elderly men playing chess. They had long white beards and seemed very wise. They were so good at chess that neither could beat the other, and the game kept going on and on.

The young man was so intrigued that he stood there and watched for what he thought was a long while. Down in the valley, he sensed the colors changing rapidly from white to green to orange, then back to white. It rotated very fast. He was so engrossed in the interesting chess game that, by the time he did come down the mountain, he discovered that centuries had passed.

When I had the goats with me near any mountains, it felt so quiet and time seemed frozen. I had to check down the mountain frequently, fearing that the same story would happen to me. Other than that, herding the sheep was one of my pastimes and I loved watching the animals and wondering about their stories.

We were forced to sell our goats a year later because my mom was tired of raising them. My heart was broken because I knew nobody else could take better care of Little Brown. One day the new owner passed by and Little Brown recognized where he was and ran right into our house. My brother and I were so excited and tried to hide him, but we were soon scolded by my mom. We felt so sad. Little Brown's eyes were begging us to let him stay with us.

It seemed so harsh to have no control over your own life; to live with no certainty. That's how I felt about animals. I secretly cried every night at the thought of Little Brown ending up on a dinner plate. I still remember his innocent eyes to this day and I didn't get over the experience for a very long time.

From Naiveté to Responsibilities

There's a part of us that never dies, it lives with us and is always inside. The beautiful things that have happened to us are all still there, waiting to be rediscovered. The relationships I had with my animal friends were among the purest I have ever known. I am so grateful for their unconditional love, and for teaching me so much.

The Undeserved Bread

I loved playing with my friends. I didn't really put much effort into study at a young age before third grade, as I didn't understand what it was for. I just enjoyed my childhood, until I was old enough to understand the situation that my family was in.

When I was 10 and in my third grade, my teacher was extremely strict; actually, she was crazy. She would beat up students if they didn't do their homework, make mistakes or not listening. She kept a metal stick close at hand and would hit a student's hands if he or she didn't behave as expected in class. This was during a time when physical abuse of children at school in China was allowed.

I was one of the students who was beaten sometimes. I was very fearful of my teacher. Whenever I thought about her, even if I was playing after school, it gave me chills and immediately saddened me. I associated studying with pain and fear because of the teacher.

One time, our school stressed the importance of the *Three Character Classic*, which is one of the classic Chinese texts. Every student was required to recite it from start to finish. It started like this: *"Men at their birth are naturally good; their natures are much the same; their habits become widely different…"*

It was long, but we were supposed to memorize it and recite it in front of the teacher and get everything right. I was nervous and lost my train of thought when my turn came, mainly because she was so strict, and I feared her so much.

Because I was unable to recite it, I was kept at school and not allowed to go home for lunch. There were a few other students in the same situation, but I was so frustrated. I hated to recite it, hated that teacher, and now I was sitting in class hungry, with no way of telling my mom that I couldn't go home for lunch. It was way past the normal time I would walk home for lunch, and my mom knew I was always punctual.

While I was trying to concentrate on my study, I suddenly saw my mom. She must have assumed that I was kept in school due to not being able to fulfill teacher's requirements. It was a common practice back then for children who did not perform well to stay longer after school without prior notice. She came to the classroom door with a piece of bread in her hand looking out for me. It was the yummy kind of bread from the store. We never bought bread because it was too expensive; we considered it a luxury. But there she was with the bread in her hand, all because I couldn't go home for lunch. Not only did she not scold me for not being able to recite the work, she even bought me a special treat.

I used to doubt if my mom really loved me, because she seemed very harsh on me. She had high moral standards for my brother and me, and we were punished with no mercy if we were ever being slightly dishonest or showed any signs of being selfish. I thought my mom would punish me for being a bad student at school. Instead she brought me goodies that I knew she was unwilling to buy on other occasions. I felt a sense of guilt and overpowering love. I wondered whether I really deserved it, but I knew without question how much my mom did love me.

From that point on, I started to put more effort into my studies. I also began to cook for our family from the age of 10. My mom was struck by her strange illness quite often and would end up in bed. From there she would give me instructions on how to cook various meals. She told me what ingredients to put in, how to make steamed buns and rice, and how to cook vegetables.

I soon become aware of the situation that I was in. I knew that my family would not be able to help me at all, and that it would all be up to me. I was the only one who could change my fate - and there seemed no other way than through education. So, I threw myself into my studies.

From Naiveté to Responsibilities

Lotus Flower Growing Through Mud

In school I was not a top student, but I was intelligent and willing to put in the work. I was also very righteous and hated violence. There were some boys in my class who bullied others; their targets were the boys whom they considered weak and a few girls. They would beat up the boys and force them to give them money or pay for their breakfast. I hated them so much. I didn't know why I hated them, as everybody else seemed to let it go or even tried to please them. I didn't understand.

When I was in fifth grade, my teacher was a talented and laid-back young man. He was certainly not crazy like my third-grade teacher. He also played with us during recess, and that's when I started to have a different view of teachers and fell in love with studying. I started to associate studying with fun instead of hate and fear.

One time he assigned us creative homework. We had to write about our dream, i.e., what we wanted to do after elementary school. We needed to write a journal about it to express our true feelings. I said in my journal that I hated those boys who bullied others and that I hoped that when I graduated from elementary school, I would not be in the same class as them. I wished that there was no bullying in the world and added that I wanted to focus all my efforts on studying.

After I had written it, I worried about it, because I thought there was too much hatred in the diary. It might be too much, considering I was only in fifth grade. I regretted "opening" my heart. How would my teacher perceive me? Would he think that I was weird or crazy? What if he told others about my hatred and intolerance? I was a little uneasy about my journal.

My teacher gave a personalized comment for every student and, when I read his comment on my journal, I was finally at peace. He praised me and said that my thinking was as pure as the lotus flower, because she grows in mud, yet is never contaminated with it. She floats on wavering water, yet never dances with it. He said I would be very successful and he was very proud of me. I remember feeling so happy to see his note; it meant a lot to me.

Yes indeed, I was growing in a "muddy" environment, but what determines the beauty of the lotus flower comes from within not without. The lotus flower never contaminated itself with the mud she grew in, and if in the clear water, she remained humble and approachable. Regardless of the environment she was in she was her own beauty. My teacher's metaphor gave me great courage and self-reassurance; it lifted up my spirit and made me appreciate my own thoughts. It meant to me that I had the ability to stay "pure" in a harsh environment and when I eventually got to an ideal environment I would stay humble and approachable.

Around this time, at age 12, I began to rise and become one of the top students. I studied harder than ever. This was when, before the start of every school year, my dad would go from house to house to borrow money for my tuition so I would never have to taste the bitterness of life that a lack of education brings like he did.

Seeing how good I was at my studies made my dad very proud. Even better, I never needed motivation since the drive came from within. He was willing to sacrifice everything he had to support me.

I saw other children with better clothes and tastier things to eat; I knew that we were different and stopped asking my parents for things. If I wanted a better situation, it was up to me to change it. And I understood that education was my only way out.

Love of Farm Work

Even though I studied hard, I was not a bookworm. My parents instilled in me the love of farm work.

I worked on the farm like a grown man. Once, when I was 13 years old, I helped out harvesting the wheat through the night, working alongside several adult men, including my dad. We worked nonstop, cutting the wheat plants down at their base, laying them in a pile and tying them together, until the entire field was cropped and packed in piles.

From Naiveté to Responsibilities

At dawn, we packed up all the wheat onto a tractor and transported it to the common ground, where the big machines were. This spacious area was well lit by big lights and was bustling throughout the night with other harvesters. There was a jovial atmosphere amongst all the neighbors, almost like a festival.

We would untie the wheat piles and feed them into the machine, which spat out the grains at one end. These we bagged, while the rest of the plant was shredded into small pieces, straw, at the other end and piled up. We would later use the straws as fuel for the stove and the huge straw pile could be used as a super slide for children.

After harvesting the whole night, I went to school without delay. Mid-term exams happened to fall on that day and I managed to do very well despite my night of labor.

Part of the reason my dad loved me so much was that I never complained about heavy farm work, but was happy to work alongside him.

I also helped out a great deal with the housework and the garden throughout elementary school and middle school. Often times, I pushed the trolley, which was as big as me, and dumped trash near a river. Some housewives were always sitting across the river playing cards, chatting, and gossiping. They saw me with the big trolley and always commented on how diligent I was. They whispered, "I wish my son would help out at home like Xu." My cheeks would flush and I would feel embarrassed, but secretly I was very flattered to hear it.

Looking back, I am very grateful that my parents instilled in me the love of work at a time other kids my age were playing princesses and princes at home. It was a priceless real-world education for me. It helped me cultivate endurance, enjoyment of hard labor, and the love of working people.

Weight on My Shoulders

As far back as I could remember, my parents had a lot of fights. My mom sometimes regretted her marriage because our family was so poor, and she couldn't see any hope. She actually considered divorce a few times when I was still young.

My mom's stepfather sometimes came to help her gather her stuff to go back home but, even though my grandma didn't agree with her daughter's marriage, she was strongly against her divorcing my dad. She didn't want the kids to end up having a stepfather and forced my mom to go back.

They would still fight from time to time though, as my mom had a short temper like her parents. The fights were always one-sided, with my mom yelling at my dad, calling him "useless," while my dad remained silent and absorbed it all in. He never argued back, because he knew that my mom had a strange illness and could relapse anytime.

My mom was frequently affected by her illness. She would suffer extreme abdominal pains. The twisting and crushing pains inside her belly was intense, and she was not able to keep any food down. It became worse when she was depressed or angry. Her illness baffled the doctors, and every exam showed that she was physically fit, yet she suffered on and off until it subsided after 10 years.

One day, when I was 11 years old, my mom was very depressed. Maybe she had had a fight with my dad. She was walking towards the mountains all by herself with sadness on her face and my dad told me, "Go get your mom, she might want to do something silly. Go and beg her to come back. You can do it." My mom had threatened to commit suicide during fights with my dad. She didn't think there was hope to get out of poverty and pain. I was frightened and worried, but not sure what I could do to help. I quickly caught up with my mom and said to her, "Mom come back. Please come back for me. We need you. I need you to come back." Luckily, she agreed.

I knew that my brother and I were the main reason for my mom to live and I had to show her that life was worth living. I had to show her that there was hope and that I could help change her life as well. I was on a mission to prove it to her. However, sometimes I felt the heaviness on my shoulders, and I felt helpless because I couldn't see the end of the tunnel. The difficulties I was facing seemed overpowering. I had cried secretly or swallowed tears many times as a young teenager. I knew that I was born into a challenging situation, and I had to do more than others to achieve my goal of getting out of poverty, with its associated pains and frustrations.

Deep down I knew that failure was not an option. I had to be successful and demonstrate to my mom that her life was worth living too. I had to figure out ways to relieve her pain and sense of hopelessness, and there was nothing better than my own action. The sense of responsibility helped to direct my life at a young age. It reassured me again and again that I was the only one who could help myself, and education was the only way out for me.

The Self-Righteous Lady

By the time I finished elementary school in my own village and entered Xinnongcun Middle School in one of the neighboring villages, I was a good, hard-working student. The school took in students from all the nearby villages, and most of us were from poor families with low social standing.

Most kids would just play, and many took great pleasure in giving the teachers headaches. They took it for granted that study was not for them and that their life was already fixed. I could see lives being wasted even at that age.

There was one boy at the school who had also been in my class since elementary school. He was naïve and upon entering middle school, he began to hang out with the "bad boys" and started smoking.

I could see where he was heading. It would be painful to see right in front of my eyes another life being wasted. I thought that he had the opportunity to choose not to hang out with the bad boys and knew that there was still time to make the decision and stay on track with good behaviors. I felt an urge to send him a warning. Smoking was the first step to becoming "bad" in my mind at that age, and I didn't want it to happen to him. However, I didn't want anyone to perceive me as minding other people's business. What if he would not take my kind warning seriously or what if he even got angry? What if others find out about it and misunderstood my note as a love letter? What if our classmates thought I was a self-righteous lady? Who was I to advise others?

I had all these "what-ifs?" running through my head and I hesitated. But on the other hand, I thought what harm could it do? It could possibly change a person's life if I provided a piece of advice at this critical time. I knew that he was a docile boy and a kind warning shouldn't get him angry. If my note was overlooked, I would simply let it go because I knew I did my part. After my internal mental battle, I finally wrote him a sincere note warning him that it would be hard for him to stop smoking once he was addicted, and that right now was the best time to quit. I advised him to stop following the "bad boys" and focus on his studies instead.

I folded the note and placed it in his desk during recess. When he saw the note, he thanked me with a genuine smile on his face, I could see hope and deep appreciation in his eyes. I was happy about what I had done. However, it only worked for a few days, and then he went back to smoking, unable to resist the gang's temptations. I felt disappointed and sad, but at the same time, I had done my part trying to help, so there were no feelings of regret of what I did.

THE MATH "GENIUS"

I became one of the few students in the school who actually studied. I was studying for dear life and rose to number one in the school. The teachers loved me.

My primary teacher was teacher Li. She was a math teacher, and she was very kind to me. I was kind of the teacher's pet. She once gave us a final math exam that was much harder than would be expected for a middle school student. I decided to take a different approach by working backward, starting from the last problem. It turned out that the last problems were the trickiest and I ended up spending 80 percent of my time on them, but they only took a third of the space. It meant that I had about 15 minutes to finish the other two thirds of the problems.

Out of frustration I decided to just use intuition and make quick decisions, barely finishing in time. When the scores came out, everybody failed except me; I got almost a perfect score and teacher Li was shocked that I had done so well.

When she revealed the answers in front of the whole class, she would purposely ask: "Who got this answer right?" Of course, I was the only one raising my hand as nobody else had solved the later problems. Teacher Li was very proud of me because, not only had I finished the test, but many of my answers went beyond the standard responses. She thought that I had an explorative mind (but I felt that it was mainly luck) and she saw in me a poor village girl who was not only intelligent, but also diligent. She wanted nothing but a bright future for me.

The Unexpected Hand-Me-Downs

My English teacher also had a big influence on me. She was much younger than teacher Li and only about 15 years older than me. She always wore nice clothes and we all knew that she was from a wealthy family in the town. Sometimes she complained about teaching in this rural area because kids were extremely mischievous and took pride in hurting teachers' feelings. It was indeed hard for her to adjust to our school.

I was among the few students she loved, and I was good at English. One time after class, she called me over and whispered, "Xu, come to my office after class." She raised her eyebrows and sounded so mysterious. I was very curious.

After class, before heading home, I went to her office. She smiled and said, "You know, I brought some clothes for you. These are all my old clothes and, if you don't mind, you can take them home and wear them." She did want to make sure that I didn't mind wearing them.

Most of my clothes up to that point were hand-me-downs; I almost never had new clothes and every teacher could tell that. My hand-me-downs were from relatives; my parents loved the idea of saving money by not buying me clothes. I never minded wearing hand-me-down clothes either because I was thrilled to have new additions to my wardrobe. But I had never had any teacher giving me clothes before, neither did I ever expect them to.

When my English teacher brought her clothes to me, I was so surprised and touched by her kindness. She knew that I came from a poor family, but I was not the typical student who gave her headaches in school. Instead I displayed kindness and understanding. She also knew that I was not a picky person. We had a great relationship, which was why she considered giving me clothes. My parents thought it was an honor that my teachers helped me out not only in my study, but also in my life.

The teachers all communicated among themselves. Later, my literary teacher also gave me some clothes. It was a small but close community and the teachers loved promising students. Teacher Li told all the other teachers my story and how poor my family was. She observed my strong will to succeed and said that I was like no other student she had seen in her decades of teaching. Because of the communications among my middle school teachers, many other teachers who didn't teach me any classes also knew about me and praised me.

The Begging for a Rare Scholarship

A rare, once-in-a-lifetime opportunity soon came my way. A group of retired wealthy people established a foundation to support children from poor villages. Their mission was to help promising students who were not able to further their education due to poor family conditions. Xinnongcun Middle School was given one spot and the chosen one would receive funds for his or her entire life's education.

We took it very seriously. In the school a lot of kids qualified in terms of the financial aspect, because most came from poor families. There were many children who were much poorer than I was, with even less money, or with handicapped parents.

However, I was one of the most promising candidates for the grant, because not only was I from a poor family, but I also studied hard. One of the most powerful officials in our school wanted to give the opportunity to the poorest student in school, but teacher Li stood up against him. She argued that they had to give the opportunity to me, because I deserved it as the most promising student. When the school official insisted, teacher Li found our school official privately and kneeled down before him, begging, crying, and telling him that they had to give it to me or else they would waste the opportunity.

Teacher Li herself came from a very poor and remote village. She had undergone many ordeals to pursue education and become a teacher. Therefore, she had great sympathy towards the children from poor families. She never tired of educating us to be better persons. Every morning she was one of the first to come to school. She used her spare time to help students catch up with their studies. She taught tirelessly and dedicated her life to the kids in the villages.

However, most kids in my class did not care about education at all. They acted against teacher Li as if going against the teacher meant that they were powerful. One of teacher Li's frequent sayings was, "There are billions of people on earth, but you guys end up in the same class and spend three years in study together. Isn't that amazing? You should cherish these years, make good friends with each other and study hard, because in the future you may end up in different parts of the world." Many kids scorned her. Indeed, our classmates came from our own village or neighboring villages within walking distance, and we had been living there for generations.

This nearsightedness clouded most people's eyes; children wasted their most promising years when they had great potential. They were not able to understand teacher Li's effort until they reached their twenties, but by then it was too late. No matter how much effort teacher Li put in, there were only a few who truly appreciated her and put effort into studying for a brighter future, and I was one of them. Therefore, teacher Li felt that it was important to kneel down in front of the school official to persuade him to give the opportunity to me instead of others.

Unfortunately, the foundation dissolved, so nothing happened. But I knew that I was so fortunate to have such a great teacher who would stand up for me like that. Later on, even after college, teacher Li and my English teacher helped me immensely, and without their financial support I would not have been able to pay off my college student loan right before coming to America. They were indeed godsends and lifelong friends. Without them, my middle school years would not have been so blessed and my career would not have been possible.

Talents are everywhere, but the people who can recognize them are rare. You might have great talents, but without the right people first recognizing them, and then helping you, it means nothing; you won't get far. One person's success is not simply his or her own effort, it has much to do with the important people behind the scenes at a time when the greatness has not yet manifested. Therefore, one should always be grateful for the people who offered a helping hand during times of hardship. I was very fortunate to have had two great teachers who recognized my potential and helped me in my times of difficulty.

Mental Note of Ambition

More opportunities soon presented themselves. At the time I had to apply for high school, China had just established a new special high school class in Beijing called Hongzhi Class. The meaning of Hongzhi is "grand ambition"; the Hongzhi class is extraordinary. It was funded by the government and was devoted to helping poor children from around the country who had demonstrated great potential and ambition.

Selected students not only had their tuition fees waived, but they received handsome monthly allowances and may have the chance to go abroad. Acceptance to such a class meant a complete life change, with great opportunities opening up.

The class was selecting only 22 students from around the country, so only the cream of the crop, with poor family backgrounds, would be accepted. The student's communication skills, social skills, personal skills and overall success were considered as well as the educational score. The competition was fierce, but it would be a great honor to be accepted.

My mom took me and her niece Xiang, who is only 40 days older than me, for the class interview in Beijing. Xiang and I both graduated from the same elementary school in our village, but since Xiang was such an excellent student, she was recommended to the best middle school in town, while I went to the neighboring village in Xinnongcun Middle School.

Xiang did very well in school and had won national writing awards. She always took important roles in school and I was never able to compete with her success.

Hundreds of students attended the Hongzhi Class interview that day. There was a long line and each of us had one-on-one time with the interviewer. Before the interview, we were given a handout containing the motto of the school, which we had to memorize. According to the motto, there were certain characteristics we needed to demonstrate in order to qualify, one of which was having great ambition.

When I was interviewed, they asked me to recite the motto. I got everything right except that I omitted the ambition part—and consequently failed the interview. I was quite upset with myself, but fortunately, my cousin Xiang got in.

From that experience, I made a mental note never again to miss being ambitious. How could I forget ambition?

Maybe it was fate that I didn't make it into Hongzhi Class. I did very well in the local high school entrance exam and, with my score, I was able to enter the best high school in town, Miyun No.2 Middle School.

Even though it was called a middle school it incorporated a high school. My cousin Xiang finished her middle school there, and I was able to follow in her footsteps and enter the high school there.

Most students in Miyun No.2 Middle School were from the central and best part of Miyun District. Only a few were from the outlying villages, because education there was so poor in the villages. If you were a village kid, your entire village would know if you got into that school, as it was considered a true honor. I felt so proud to be the only student accepted from my village that school year.

Chapter 3

Rewards to My Ambition

随心 *(Sui Xin) means to fulfill one's true heart desires as one wishes. When there's a conflict between what others think about what you should do and your passion, always follow your inner callings. It takes courage to follow your true heart desires but it is the fuel for your success. This chapter is about how I got into one of the top universities in China and how I was determined to embrace challenges.*

My Family During High School

I was assigned to one of the best high school classes in Miyun No.2 Middle School. There were a few other students from surrounding villages attending as well.

At this time, my mom's health had improved so much that she was able to work as a housemaid, taking care of an elderly lady around the clock. My dad worked as a gatekeeper for a factory, so he wasn't home much either.

My brother Kai was chosen from our elementary school to join a professional weightlifting team in the town, so he lived on campus there. However, his bone development lagged behind, so his coach couldn't really let him lift weights and eventually decided to dismiss him from the team. My mom begged the coach to let him stay, because that way he could stay in the town and get into the associated middle school there, instead of Xinnongcun Middle School. The town offered a much better education and seemed the only option for my brother to have a bright future.

Despite my mom's appeals, the coach stood by his decision. So, my mom went to his house to plead. The coach wasn't home, but his wife received my mom. She was also a weightlifting coach on the same sports team and my mom kneeled down in front of her, begging her to let my brother stay. She told the coach's wife how we came from a poor family, and that if my brother went back to the village, he would have no future. The pleas worked, and the coach ended up breaking the rules and letting my brother stay on the team so that he could get a better education.

Kai lived on campus with the weightlifting team. My family was thus split into four different locations, and there wasn't much need for me to go home during my high school years. It was a 35-minute bike ride each way, so I boarded at my high school, like many other kids from the remote villages.

In the beginning, I was a bit sad that my family had to split into different places, and I would be all by myself. I was afraid that there was not much sense of a family anymore; I missed the closeness of a family. There was some feeling of lack of protection. But I understood that my parents were doing the best they could to make a living and supporting my brother and me.

Apart from being a little sad, I was more excited for something new. I was looking forward to a new environment of living away from my parents with new friends. I thought that it could be a good thing for me to develop new skills and learn from others.

This turned out well, because I had seven amazing girls as roommates. They also came from remote villages, unlike the vast majority of my schoolmates who were from the center of the town. Coming from a rural background, my roommates were diligent like me; we had a lot in common. Despite the fact that boarding students comprised only a small percentage of all the students in Miyun No.2 Middle School, boarding students were extra diligent and a lot more independent. Looking back, I was glad that I boarded in high school, as it taught me many important things that I would not have gotten in other ways.

Boarding Life

The boarding years in high school were very helpful to me. It was the first time I left home for extended periods of time and I learned to be more independent. I could not depend on my parents or relatives for everything, but had to focus on building new, trusting relationships. Teamwork was also a great skill that I learned during this time.

My roommates and I took turns to fetch hot water from our water house on campus for our daily needs. We took turns cleaning our dorm. Our dorm supervisors scored our tidiness multiple times a day and the scores were pooled to the general scores of the entire class, so it was a very serious matter to keep clean and organized. Often times, we sat at the same table and ate together in the cafeteria, especially on weekends when the campus was so quiet. We formed a special bond. We cared about each other and we knew what was going on with our roommates. We always helped each other as much as we could. For example, one of my roommates went on a diet for weeks trying to lose weight the unhealthy way, but the rest of us were very concerned about her and tried to help her with self-image issues. We cared about each other deeply. Our dorm supervisors would shut off the electricity inside the dorm building at ten o'clock sharp in the evenings, so our studies had to be done before that time. We learned to become efficient and get our things done on time. With eight girls in the same dorm, we learned tolerance, understanding, and caring for each other.

When you are placed on a team or a group you get to learn how to interact with others, and understand and support each other. You will learn that it is not all about you but the group as a whole. If the group as a whole is healthy and inspiring, each member will benefit greatly. The sum of the whole is far more than the addition of each member. The boarding experience in high school years was instrumental in developing my sense of a group and teamwork.

I tried to save as much money as I could in high school. Sometimes I would just buy a steamed bun from the cafeteria without any veggies, because I didn't want to spend too much money. The way I looked at it was that all I needed to do was to fill my stomach, so I gave up on nutrition.

My aunt whose name was Xiuqin, worked for a while at the school as a chef in a temporary cafeteria for construction workers who were renovating there. Her job was part of the compensation she received after her husband (my dad's older brother) died in a construction accident at the age of 38.

One day I was walking on campus and I saw my aunt. She said: "Why not come to my cafeteria to save money on your food?" I went there for lunch with her and other construction workers. She gave me good food and vegetables, and told me to feel free to come have lunch with her at any time.

Later, she told my mom that when she was walking on the campus, she was expecting to see all kids from decent families. When she saw a very poor girl approach from a distance, she was wondering who she was and how she could be in such a great school. As I got closer, she suddenly realized it was me, and felt immediate pity. That's why she invited me to eat in her cafeteria for free.

Aunt Xiuqin was very kind to me. She knew that I was a good girl and was being frugal, so she wanted to help out. Every little bit did help, and I appreciated it.

I studied hard in high school, partly because I didn't really have anything better to do. All my friends studied really hard as well. It seemed that, because we were from poor areas, we had to work doubly hard because education was our only way out for a brighter future. We were quite aware of that and would go to the library together to study until late, every single day. It was a great environment for me, because I didn't feel like an outcast like I did in middle school, where I was the only student who wanted to study, and I had to deal with so many distractions because of it.

We often times imitate what others do, especially those around us. We may not even question it but simply blend in, and do as others do. I often thought that what makes a school, a company or any other organizations good isn't as much about the organization per se but about the environment/culture and the people to whom you are exposed. They have subtle but profound impacts as to how you will behave and develop your beliefs; they may help expand your awareness, stretch your limits, or be detrimental to your development. We are greatly molded by those closest to us. I was grateful that I had the opportunity to mingle with excellent high school students from town and it helped me cultivate a good habit of studying, as well as understanding others.

Look at the people you are friends with, you will find out much about yourself. Be vigilant about whom you interact with, purposely seek out crowds that are beneficial for your personal development and mingle with those who can lift you up.

Family Tension and Another Lesson

One time when I went back home for a brief visit, nobody was home, so I decided to visit my uncle, my dad's younger brother. His house was the original family house of the big family, which he inherited because he was his parents' favorite. However, he and his wife didn't support my grandparents in old age, as is our cultural tradition. Instead, my grandparents lived with my family right up until their deaths. My grandparents even had to sue my uncle to force him to share the responsibility of supporting them.

I felt a little awkward visiting my uncle, because he wasn't close to the rest of the family. And I certainly didn't like how he and his wife treated my grandparents. They seemed selfish and cruel, even though my parents taught me never to pass judgment on my superiors.

When I arrived at my uncle's, his wife was cooking dinner in another room. My uncle swiftly took out 20 Yuan and gave it to me and said, "You know, you are boarding at the high school, no one's taking care of you and I want to give you some money so you can buy some good food for yourself. I know you are always a good student and I really want to help you."

But I refused his money. Perhaps I didn't trust him or maybe it felt like a bribe. It just didn't feel right to take his money. He insisted on giving me the cash. I guessed he might have felt guilty that he hadn't really helped my family in hard times, and that because I was such a good girl, he thought he should help me a little. After the money went back and forth between us for a while, I finally pushed it under the couch, where it was impossible to reach.

I could feel that he was trying to be a good uncle. As he grew older, he started seeing the value of staying close to his family and he became more sentimental every time I saw him.

Sometimes it takes time for people to learn valuable lessons and to be nice to others, even if those others are your family members.

An Ambitious University Application

High school flew by quickly. With good friends as roommates and classmates, all my energy was spent on study or physical exercise. Life was simple, but despite my great efforts, I was never a top student.

When the time came to apply to colleges, each of us needed to select three colleges as our top priority, second priority and third priority, respectively. I wanted to enter a teaching school and I chose Beijing Normal University (BNU) as my first priority, because it was the best teaching university in China. It had a great reputation in the teaching profession, and I was under the impression that girls should either become a teacher or a nurse to have a bright future.

Becoming a teacher or nurse was perceived as appropriate and respected professions for women, to the point it was expected of Chinese girls to become a teacher or nurse. On hearing what I applied, one of my high school classmates, a top male student, "complimented" me by saying, "Becoming a teacher is good enough for girls! You are on the right track." I felt the condescending tone in his voice and I didn't quite like his "praise" of me. It's almost as if girls were supposed to take what was wrongly considered easier professions due to low expectations.

Since it was such an important decision for our futures, our teacher examined everyone's selections of schools carefully, making sure that they were appropriate. It was very critical to set the priorities right because if you were not accepted by the university you set as your first priority, then your scores and files would be forwarded to the university that was your second priority.

You would not be considered by the second priority unless the university was unable to fill up with applicants who set the school as their first priority. If you were not chosen by your second priority your files would then be forwarded to the university you set as your third priority, where you have even less competitive edge. It was therefore extremely important that you were able to get into the university you set as your primary priority. If you missed out, you could end up in a bad school.

When my teacher saw my top priority, he thought that I aimed too high. BNU was very competitive and it was becoming one of the top universities in China. Bright applicants from the entire country competed to get in there and only the top students from my school should consider it, and that certainly didn't include me.

He recommended that I change my top priority to Capital Normal University instead. It was a decent teaching university, and even though it was ranked lower than BNU, it was much less competitive to get in. I would stand a good chance to secure my future.

I thought my teacher's advice made sense. If I set Capital Normal University as my second priority, I might not be able to get in if I failed my ambitious first priority, so I followed his recommendation and changed my top priority to Capital Normal University.

After I made the change, something didn't feel quite right. I suddenly had the thought, "Why am I giving up before I have even tried?" Sure, there was a risk involved, but there was nothing wrong in giving it a try and I'd never accomplish anything if I feared taking a risk. Why deprive myself of the chance? My inner voice was questioning me, challenging me. It just didn't feel right to lower my expectations because of what others thought about me. Some part of me was being very feisty and ambitious.

So, at the very last minute, I changed my top priority back to BNU and prepared to face the consequences.

An Escape Route and a New Struggle

I didn't heap too much pressure on myself for the college entrance exam because I didn't have any preconceived notions of whether I would succeed or fail. It was just like taking a regular exam and I would deal with the results afterwards, whatever happened.

I tried the best I could and when my score came out, it was decent without being exceptional. It gave me a chance of being accepted by BNU, but I was not too confident. My future was up in the air.

But in mid-summer 2001, I received the acceptance letter from BNU! My mom was so thrilled that she put down her knitting and lifted me up in the air, laughing with joy. I didn't know where she got the strength, but she was just so proud. I've never seen my mom so happy before.

Our family would have its first college student, and everyone was very proud. What they saw for me was light at the end of the tunnel, a potential escape route from the poverty that generations had been confined to. I knew that this was a new beginning.

On the first day of college, September 8, 2001, teacher Li drove my parents and me to BNU. I got settled in my new dorm, saw new faces, and met new people. When we got familiar with each other later on, we compared scores, and that's when I realized that my score was the lowest in my class, except for some students with special talents. I had been so lucky to get in, as I was right at the cut-off point for being accepted.

Even more amazingly, my major was biology, which was one of the hottest majors back then.

I couldn't fathom, nor did I want to, where I would wind up if I failed my top priority. I was beyond grateful that I could step into the door of BNU. Most importantly, I trusted myself and went beyond what was expected of me. I was secretly proud of myself being able to make the right choices under pressure and remain ambitious.

When the situation is tough, when you can't see what's beyond, when the challenge is right in your face, that's when you needed to trust yourself the most. Because no one knows you better than you do. Whatever others say about you are their perceptions of you, not your true talents and abilities. When there is a conflict between others' expectations and your passion, always follow your inner callings.

Oftentimes, with what seems like bold actions, you get handsome rewards. Think about how many people were stopped by potential failures and sought the alternative easy route instead, whereas they could have accomplished something amazing. You can't succeed unless at least you try. If we can all foresee the future, we would all take the risks; in fact, there would be no risks at all.

What will make you stand out is the ability to take the actions regardless of the fear of the unknown, which includes the possibilities of failures. Otherwise you will deprive yourself of the possibility of being successful. The future is unknown, but you must take actions and corresponding risks now to get to your desirable future, and in this process failure could be a result but you don't entertain this possibility and feed its power. You forge ahead fearlessly.

My college classmates were all the best of the best from educated families in different states around the country. I was under no illusions about the situation that I was in, and the pressure that was on me. I knew I needed to work hard to catch up to my classmates, many of whom I looked up to. This was something I was prepared to do. I was lucky enough to get into BNU with amazing environments and surrounded by talents from all over the country in China. I was not about to waste the chance.

College Culture and Lonely Days

I worked hard in college, but still I was a mediocre student. The seven other girls in my dorm all got higher scores, and they studied hard, too. We always worked as a team. We would go to classes early in the morning and reserve seats for our roommates so that we got the best seating. Most of my classmates were very eager for knowledge, and the classroom atmosphere was super positive. BNU lived up to its reputation and had a high quality of teaching and learning, and I was very grateful to be in such an environment. I saw the thirst for knowledge everywhere on campus.

My roommates were all well-rounded people. They were great at singing, social skills, and many other things that I lacked, as well as being great at studying. I really enjoyed learning from everyone and I respected them all. I was a quieter type and didn't talk much. We treated each other as sisters during the college years, and we were very close.

Sometimes we would talk late into the night, and occasionally go out together to restaurants or karaoke. It was interesting to see how the personalities of eight girls from different parts of the country could blend by being thrown into the same dorm at college. It almost felt like there was a micro-culture within our dorm, a fostering environment where we helped each other learn and laugh in those memorable four years. I had invited my roommates to my house one time for sleepover and we spent the day hiking into mountains and later made yummy dumplings together. We had lots of fun talking, laughing and even making fun of each other. We were like a family in that we not only cared about each other's studies but also our personal lives. It was a real sisterhood that has lasted a lifetime. We were in touch even after we were separated into different parts of the world.

Some friendships you will never forget. Even though years or even decades pass and each of you is busy with your own life, when you reconnect it feels like the times you spent together were just yesterday. There is a deep sense of trust. No matter how much has changed about you and your life, your friends are wishing you the best you could be and live in your heart always.

I didn't go home much during college because I figured I couldn't change my family's situation by my physical presence. The only way I could help was by spending every minute I could on doing well in my studies. Only by changing my own future could I change my family's.

On weekends, I would tutor high school and middle school children, mainly teaching them math and English. I was able to make some money to cover part of my living expenses. College tuition was covered by my student loan, so my family didn't need to worry about it.

Some of the kids I tutored had nice families. One middle-class family whose daughter I tutored knew that I came from a poor family and they would invite me to stay for dinner with them after each session, which was nice of them.

One cold winter day near Chinese New Year, I decided to stay on campus to earn some cash from tutoring. It was a tradition to celebrate Chinese New Year with family, so almost everybody went back home and the campus was scarily quiet. I felt a little sad and lonely, but I thought I might as well make some money rather than go home and be another mouth to feed for my parents.

I felt like I was slaving myself though, and I felt a heavy weight on my shoulders. I regretted a little not going home for the warmth and festive time together with my family. After one tutoring session that wintertime, it was very cold riding my bike back to campus. The bike lane on the highway was watery and a cleaner was sweeping the water off the road as I passed. She could not have seen me and splashed water all over me.

First, I was upset and felt sorry for myself, but I immediately calmed down. I was soaking wet, it was as if the fire in me was being quenched, but I wouldn't allow it. I had made the choice to not go home, but to focus on improving my situation while others were celebrating a significant holiday. The choice I made was serious and it was about my endurance and my will for a change of fate. I should welcome the consequences and enjoy every step of the way. Being splashed by dirty water, and perhaps other mishaps and challenges down the road, were surely things that would cross my path, therefore I had no reason to complain but to embrace it fully and understand the strength of my own will. I became so peaceful, clear and grateful for what had happened. It was a reminder for me to stay strong and stand by my own decisions.

I know how it feels to be caught up in a life so hopeless that sometimes the obstacles seem too big to get around. But if you push through the pain and embrace what comes about along your journey, you can achieve what seems unobtainable. Instead of being crushed by challenges and difficulties, use these as a reminder of how great you are. You are determined to get what you want, despite all the challenges.

View the challenges as tests from the Universe to see if you really want what you say you want. Be grateful for the obstacles, difficulties, and roadblocks, for they are the very things to make you stronger in your pursuit of your dreams. Remember, how you view things, people and circumstances are completely your choice. You can turn any 'bad' situations into positive ones inside your mind, and it will propel you towards achieving your dreams.

I returned home only around five times in the four years of college, even though it was only two hours by bus. Every time I went back, my dad would hold my hand and walk in the street with me and ask me what I wanted, like when I was a young kid. He still treated me as his princess.

Then, when I had to go back to school, he would ride his motorcycle and send me off to the bus station in town. I became sentimental each time I left, but I presented a brave face to my dad, waving him to go back, telling him not to worry about me and that I would be absolutely fine.

As soon as I turned my head away, tears started streaming down my face. They were not tears of hopelessness but of determination. Every time I went back home I was reminded why I wanted to work hard, why I was on a mission to change my own fate and that of my family. When I was leaving home for school, I reflected upon my life and how far I had gone. I thought about how my parents supported me despite our poverty. I thought about how incredible I was to embark on a mission that's bigger than me. My mission was yet to be accomplished. My heart would not settle until I'd steered my family's fortunes in a better direction, whenever that day may come.

First College Crush

There were 80 students in my class, about a third of whom were boys, since BNU was a teaching school that was dominated by girls. I got along well with everybody and was not jealous when I saw the girls having dates that made them so happy. I daydreamed about having a boyfriend who loved me.

Sometimes I found myself longing for a relationship, but I wasn't in luck. Few people paid attention to me; I was quiet, shy and ordinary-looking.

I ended up not having a romantic relationship in college. Not that I didn't want one, it was just that no one really took to me. Perhaps that was a good thing, looking back.

I did like one boy who was a graduate student at the time, and who was five years older than me. I had a crush on him because he was handsome and a well-rounded person. His boss was in America, so he was the boss in charge of the whole biology lab. I felt that he was a leader and I admired him.

I would try to get close to him. Of course, he treated me as a naïve girl and maybe he thought I wasn't pretty, or he didn't like my family background, or maybe I just wasn't his type. I was a bit insecure, fearing that he could see through my naivety.

I heard that he loved a delicate and aloof girl in his lab. She came from a very wealthy family. She looked quite frail to me, but I got it. He liked that type, not someone like me. Perhaps he wanted to be someone who protects his lover, in that sense she suited him. There weren't many real interactions between me and him other than seeing him as a superior who I looked up to.

The Planting of a Seed

While in my junior year in college we started to plan for our futures. At that time, a new institution was founded called the National Institute of Biological Sciences (NIBS). It was directed by one of our alumni who became a famous American scientist. NIBS was recruiting many top college students for its graduate school, as it aimed to become one of the best in China in the field of biology.

About a third of my classmates were recommended, without needing any exams. There was sufficient funding as China was growing into one of the top countries in the world for biological sciences. NIBS offered good benefits compared to other conventional graduate schools.

I'd already decided to pursue higher studies in biology, but I wasn't sure where to apply yet. I sought advice from the graduate student who I was fond of, since he was more experienced. He said, "If you want to be a real scientist you should go to America. It has the best science. You can have a bright future there."

I agreed, but partly because getting a PhD in America might make me feel more equal to him. Perhaps he would look up to me? At the same time, I knew that it was just a dream.

However, it slowly dawned on me that there was no better way to change one's future than by going abroad. I disliked the bureaucracy in China and the fact that poor people had very limited opportunities to change their lot, so that first mention of America by the graduate student planted a seed.

At the same time, I understood the huge risks involved with aiming to go to the US. It was just a year after 9/11 and America was very strict about foreign students. There was also limited funding available for conducting scientific research. In addition, the majority of Chinese students who went there for PhD studies already had a master's degree from China, which meant that they had three more years' hands-on experience than a fresh face from college like me.

Students with master's degrees had strong academic backgrounds, experimental skills, and some were even published. How could I compete with them and with other top Chinese college students who wanted to go abroad after college? I was just an average student at BNU, and the chances of making it seemed so slim as to be negligible.

There was another risk too, if I was going to pursue this dream. Because of the timing, if I failed in the mission to get to the US, I would have missed the opportunity to be recommended to NIBS. The doors would be closed on me.

So, I had the choice of reaching for a great goal with a slim chance of success or settling for a much more achievable, but lesser goal.

Chapter 4

Passage to America

毅力 *(Yi Li) is the Chinese word for determination, perseverance, and tenacity. It means hang on to your dreams and do not give up no matter what happens. It is the power that enabled me to accomplish my seemingly impossible dream of coming to America. Through conquering the ordeals on the journey, I learned this important lesson: Where there is a WILL there is a way.*

Listening to My Inner Voice

I was totally aware that it was a huge risk to take to try to go abroad, but deep down I felt I should try. Just like I had tried for BNU and got in, when the safer option had been to apply elsewhere.

No matter how unlikely it was, I decided on bold action, cutting off all routes to other possibilities until I felt that I had no other choice but to follow my dream. But before doing so, I made a deal with myself that, even if I failed, I would not regret it at all. I planned on accepting the worst result, failure, so there was nothing else that could stop me. I knew that I would face ordeals on this path that I had chosen, but I decided to burn the ships and make my mission non-negotiable. I was fully determined and absolutely committed.

At that time, some of my classmates also decided to apply to go abroad to study. Many had had this dream since they were very little. They came from much wealthier and more educated families, some with parents who were professors in universities. Some had even been abroad already.

And there was me, who had never even ventured out of Beijing, staying most of my life in one local village and town. I had no foundation to go abroad and so most people considered my goal to be a daydream. That included my roommates, who tried to talk me out of it and who urged me to be more realistic. I understood that they were trying to prevent me from ruining my future, and I appreciated their concerns, but my mind was made up. It was time to make my dream a reality.

Like most of my classmates, I had already received all my credits at BNU, and I didn't need to attend any classes in my senior year. The last year was intended for fieldwork, if we chose to be teachers. All my roommates had their futures secured. Some were recommended to NIBS and others were recommended to PhD studies in our department, without needing any exams. They were all awesome students. After years of studying hard, finally they had time to breathe and just enjoy life for a while: relaxing, watching movies in the dorm, or hanging out with friends. They had every reason to celebrate and I so wished I could do that too.

I felt so down, because I was the only one having to continue to work hard. By the time I made the decision to apply to American graduate schools, I only had three months left to prepare for the Graduate Record Examinations (GRE) test, which I would need to pass in order to go abroad right after college the next year, in 2005.

Unlike many of my classmates who had been studying GRE since high school, I had never touched it before. I felt the pressure and, to keep my mind on my studies, I moved out of my dorm, away from the celebrations and cheers.

I rented a basement apartment under the chemistry department on our campus. It was a place for the chefs, cleaners, and other workers at school. I lived there for a few months while I was preparing for the test. During the day, I would find a classroom for study, and at night return to the apartment to sleep. My life consisted of two dots with a line in between.

One of my classmates helped me assemble my first computer. It was a bulky desktop. I started to learn how to use it to type. I also got my first email address, even though I didn't really have any need to send anybody emails yet. I was preparing myself for the near future, when I would need technology.

A Stranger's Help...and No Fear of Failure

On the day of my GRE test it started pouring, and I experienced complicated feelings. I understood that it was a very important day for me. The day had finally come, a day I had been expecting, and dreading at the same time. How will it go? Will I do well on the exam? Will I be able to achieve this seemingly impossible dream and make it to America? I was a bit apprehensive, feeling the significance of the day accompanying the pouring rain. I was strolling on campus without an umbrella. How could I even get to the examination place without being soaked? I had no umbrella and I certainly wasn't thrilled with the rain on this important day. Why was the weather not cooperating? Was it a sign that I would fail? Did the rain indicate tears later on for me? I tried not to think that way, but I had to get an umbrella to get to the exam.

Suddenly, I saw a man riding a bike, holding his umbrella. I stopped him and asked to borrow his umbrella so I could go to the GRE examination place. I felt ashamed because it seemed selfish of me to ask such a question while the guy needed his umbrella too. It was not typical of me to make this unabashedly rude request, but I know that I needed to go above and beyond my comfort zone and what is perceived as common sense. Taking bold actions is what I needed to do to achieve unbelievable success. I needed to ask for help along the way, even from total strangers, without feeling guilty. With this thinking, I was able to sum up the courage to stop a stranger and ask for his umbrella.

Luckily for me, he was very kind. He smiled, and generously handed me his umbrella. I asked where I should return it after the test and he told me that he worked at the red building right in front of us. I was so relieved to make it to the test, and afterwards, when I returned the umbrella, I told him about my dream of going abroad. He smiled with admiration and encouraged me to reach for my dream. Even though I didn't find out his name and I wouldn't recognize him now, I was grateful beyond words that a total stranger would help me out and be understanding of my dream, at one of the most difficult times of my life.

It took about six weeks to get our scores back, but it felt like an eternity. Finally, the results were released, and mine was 480 out of 800. I felt like I had been struck by lightning; it was simply not acceptable! All the hard work was meaningless now, as I felt the bubble of hope burst inside me. It would be impossible to get into any school with that score. My classmates, who had also taken the GRE test, fared much better than I did, but they still considered their scores not competitive enough. Did that mean I failed? I remembered my own promise to myself that I would not embrace regret even if I failed. Now I did fail, should I accept the reality now?

I felt that I hit the bottom. I didn't know what to do.

Even classmates with much higher GRE scores than me gave up on their dreams of going abroad, and went with NIBS. It seemed like a smart move. I could have followed suit and requested a chance to be recommended to NIBS too. After all, that would have meant a very secure future. And a PhD from NIBS would provide a much higher chance of going abroad in the future, so many of my classmates took that approach.

But after a few days, I mentally accepted my GRE score, and thought that maybe it was not the end of the world, after all. Nowhere did it say that I couldn't apply for graduate school in the US with that score. If I didn't try, how would I know?

Since I burned the ship and made the deal to myself that even if I failed I would not regret it, that meant there was nothing to lose and I would not blame myself for any undesirable outcome. Getting to know my GRE score does not equal failure, because that's not rejections from schools after all. I realized that I still had a chance to make it, and I would not give up until I exhausted the possibilities. Therefore, I persisted where others gave up. I didn't know where the future lay, but I wanted to forge ahead and find out.

Finding a Way

I quickly picked myself up and started preparing for the upcoming TOEFL (Test of English as a Foreign Language) test. After that was done, I could finally take time to breathe.

I thought about the situation that I was in. I was certain that I would fail to secure a place in the US by conventional means. No one would take me on as a graduate student because of my average college scores, my poor GRE result, and without the experimental backgrounds that were required of my major. I was still waiting for my TOEFL score to come out, but based on how I had done up to that point, it became clear to me that I needed to do something bold.

Scores do indicate knowledge and abilities to some extent, but it is not the whole story about a person. I believed that there were many great qualities beyond the measurement of numbers that determine a person's potential and ability, such as imagination, tenacity, and positivity. I wondered who would look beyond the scores? Who would look beyond the numbers and evaluate the student as a whole being? And how could I make the connection to such a person, if he or she exists?

I figured that such a person should be located in one of the best universities in the United States because such universities may have higher tendencies to consider breaking the norm and recognize talents in different forms beyond what appears on the surface. I felt an urgency to reach out and find this person and make a deep connection. There had to be a way.

I looked up universities such as Harvard and the like. I found the top professors and read their life stories as much as I could. When I felt there was a match and a potential connection, I would send out an email, expressing my desire to work in their labs.

One day, while I was browsing, I came across a picture of a professor who looked so young. It was a black and white picture on a university website, and I remember thinking that the professor looked very kind. The university was new to me. It was called Wesleyan and the professor looking back at me did cell death studies.

Cell death was a hot topic in 2004, and I thought that this was what I really wanted to study. However, because I had never heard of the school I almost dismissed it as not worth pursuing. But it would not hurt to send an email, even if it didn't sound like a "top" university.

I found the young professor's email address on the website and sent him a message. I first told him where I found his info and why I wanted to join his lab to study cell death as a graduate student. It was short and to the point. The next day I received his kind reply. He said that at this stage of his life he was not accepting new graduate students, but he recommended two professors from his department who I should contact.

I took a second look and realized that his photo on the website was probably taken before I was born! I figured that he must be close to retiring now, so I looked up the two names he gave me. One was a male professor and the other one a female, both from Wesleyan University in Middletown, Connecticut.

I thought that the woman, named Jan Naegele, might resonate with me better and be able to understand my life story. I chose her to send an email to. I first told her that the other professor in her department had recommended her to me, and then expressed my desire to join her lab as a graduate student, and that I was looking forward to her reply.

To my surprise, Jan replied me the next day, saying that she was coming to Beijing in two weeks and would like to interview me! She said that she was accompanying a team of Yale professors, and that they would visit Shanghai and then briefly Beijing. She said she would email me the hotel name and the date we should meet up once she was in Beijing. I couldn't believe it! I was so excited. I really felt like the Universe was listening to me and it seemed like a once-in-a-lifetime opportunity.

When you are not confined by what the "facts" (scores, odds, and rigid cultures) tell you and reach out to your dreams fearlessly, the Universe will arrange itself to create "coincidences" and bring on the right people at the right time. Had I not followed my true feelings I could have given up my dream of going abroad, because I got a horrible score and it seemed logical to give up. The way the Universe helps you may not seem obvious for you, therefore what you need here is trust and to follow your inner callings.

Instead of hampered by roadblocks and difficulties, see them as challenges the Universe put out for you. The Universe is asking you, do you really want what you said you wanted? The way the Universe tests your true intent is by placing obstacles in front of you, and its purpose is to make you stronger to carry out your mission in life. Don't be afraid to take bold action, and trust the Universe and your own abilities at all times. Only by doing so will you achieve amazing results.

Many people fear that they would fail, therefore they do not even take the first steps necessary to succeed. What they are waiting on is absolute certainty that they *will* succeed, which never comes. What you need instead is the ability to conquer fear, so that you can take action even when you don't see all the steps.

Fear is the opposite of love. When you know that the Universe loves you unconditionally and wants you to succeed in good deeds, you will become fearless and make the effort to achieve your personal success. Your success not only propels you personally, but it also demonstrates to others what is really possible for them and it helps push humanity forward, however small that is. Therefore, the Universe has the best interest in your success, and you just need to trust it and take corresponding actions!

The Meeting That Almost Never Happened

When Jan got to Beijing, she sent me the name of the hotel she was staying at and the date we would meet up in a couple days. I looked up the hotel name she gave me and discovered that there were quite a few hotels with the same name in Beijing. I tried to locate the exact one she would be staying at, but the day before our supposed meeting, I still wasn't able to figure it out and I was not able to reach her via email due to her traveling.

On a cold and windy day in October 2004, I rode my bike from hotel to hotel, trying to find the one Jan might be staying in. I asked the receptionists if they had an American professor named Jan Naegele registered, but none recognized her name in their systems.

I was so frustrated and felt that I was losing the grip on my one big chance. Could it end like this? What would happen next so that I could connect with her, or would I ever? It was close to eleven o'clock the night before I was supposed to meet up with Jan, and I still couldn't get in touch with her because her name did not show up in any hotel registries. I called hotel after hotel asking for her name again, sadly to no avail. Finally, I decided to dial the last number before going to bed and letting go of the whole interview thing. Perhaps it was not supposed to happen.

I thought it through again: she was from Wesleyan, which seemed like a smallish university. It was unlikely that her school had been invited to China. She did mention that she was accompanying a team from Yale. Could it be that her husband was from Yale and that's why she was in China?

By that logic, her name might not be on the record but her husband's instead; and, since they were US professors whose trip might be sponsored, it was reasonable that they were staying at the best hotel with the name I was given.

I dialed the best hotel with the name Jan had given me. I asked the receptionist to look up the record for Yale professors to see if there was anyone who could possibly be related to a woman named Jan Naegele.

With a short delay the receptionist connected me to a room, where a man answered the phone. I knew it must be Jan's husband. I asked for Jan and he asked me to wait a second and he would go and fetch her from another room, since she was chatting with friends.

I finally got in touch with Jan at the eleventh hour! We confirmed the exact time to meet up in the hotel lobby the next day. Just when I thought it was never going to happen suddenly everything fell into place. What a relief! I was able to call it a day and went to bed.

The next morning, I rode my bike all the way to the hotel; the route was already so familiar. We met in the lobby and I felt a little nervous since I had never really talked to any foreigners. My English up to that point was mostly for taking exams and I felt that my verbal English was not great. It was a little intimidating for me, but I quickly calmed down, because Jan seemed so kind and loving. She was about my mom's age and she was very graceful. I figured that, as a female professor herself, she must have a great understanding of my situation.

My nervousness disappeared, and I even joked how I had been running all over the city trying to find her hotel the day before. I shared with her my childhood stories and how I overcame difficulties in life and how I was determined to change my own fate. She asked me a lot of questions along the way about my life, my family and my studies. She nodded with sympathy as I was telling my story. I was surprised that she could understand me so well, despite the cultural differences and my not-so-good English.

She asked me for my GRE score. I told her and immediately saw the disappointment in her face, which saddened me. She said that her school was very competitive. It was a small liberal university, and they only accepted a few international students, so only the cream of the crop could get in.

She said that my score was too low. After I told her that I had also taken TOEFL, she said that I should let her know the score once it came out and that we should keep in touch and see how things go.

Despite her negative reaction to my GRE score, which I was quite ashamed of, I was quite happy with how my interview with Jan went. I felt so much better for my future now that I had at least been interviewed by a US professor. That seemed like an important first step towards going abroad and I especially appreciated Jan's understanding of my family's situation, and her kindness in meeting with me.

Keeping The Dream In Sight

My TOEFL score was decent. I emailed Jan and told her, and she was happy. She reminded me however, that, to get into Wesleyan, I needed to have some "wet lab" experience. All I had to that point was washing dishes and cleaning laboratories; not nearly enough. She suggested that I find a biology lab where I could do some volunteer work to get some hands-on experience.

Since I was just a senior in college and I wasn't planning to do my PhD in China, it was hard for me to find a lab. There seemed no point in training me if I wasn't going to further my study there.

I kept contacting top labs in Beijing and, before long, my persistence paid off. I found a kind woman professor named Dr. Feng who was in her sixties. She was an excellent researcher and her experiments had even been carried out by Chinese Space Program in outer space. Even though she had already retired by the time I contacted her, she still ran a lab and was very active in the Institute of Zoology (IOZ) in the Chinese Academy of Sciences. The Academy consisted of a series of institutes including IOZ, and it was considered one of the most reputable science institutions in the country. Both Dr. Feng and her husband were esteemed scientists in China.

Once accepted, I moved to a location closer to the Institute. At that time, the IOZ was close to Tsinghua University, one of the top two universities in China. Therefore, I rented a basement apartment on campus, because I didn't want to lose touch with the school culture. I felt safe there, plus I could use the classrooms for night studies and the playground for running, a habit that I had kept since high school. I had a high school friend who was studying in Tsinghua and he helped me settle down in my new place.

A new life started for me inside Dr. Feng's lab. Everyone there was either a Master or PhD student. I was the youngest, but I blended in well. Everyone was very nice to me, like big sisters and brothers, and they taught me many skills. Many of them wanted to go abroad too after they finished their degrees, and they admired my courage to try to go to America right after college. Dr. Feng was very kind to her students, including me. She herself had studied abroad during her younger years and she displayed an open-mindedness that was rare of women her age in China.

Making Ends Meet and Finding Unexpected Support

However, life continued to be tough for me. I was struggling to make ends meet. I wasn't able to continue my tutoring and had no source of income. I borrowed money from friends and cousins to pay for my rent and meals (which were always easy and cheap). I would go to street vendors and buy two steamed buns with vegetables inside. It cost less than two Yuan a meal and I always tried to get buns with different varieties of vegetables inside, so that I maintained some nutritional balance.

Rent was my biggest expense. Even my small apartment inside Tsinghua cost about 500 Yuan a month, which was a lot to me. I was trying to figure out ways to reduce that expense, as all I really needed was a bed to sleep in at the end of the day.

Luckily one of my friends in Dr. Feng's lab offered a solution. She said that her best friend was on a field trip in another state, and her apartment was vacant, so I could move in. I hesitated, but she reassured me that her friend was very easy going and that she wouldn't mind me moving in to save money. With my friend being such a great person, and knowing that she really sympathized with my situation, I gratefully agreed and terminated my rental agreement at Tsinghua.

The day I was supposed to move into the new apartment, my friend suddenly told me that I could no longer move in, because her friend was very upset with the arrangement. Hearing this I was completely shocked and didn't know where I could go. I thought an apartment had been lined up, but all of a sudden, I didn't have anywhere to move in. I felt like I was leaping without a net. I was terrified. Where would I be sleeping? Could I be homeless? I spent the whole morning in distress.

It was a very cold winter's day in 2004. It started snowing around noon, while everyone was rushing home for lunch or heading to the cafeteria. I was walking down the stairs of the research building, blankly staring into space, not knowing what to do or where to go. Just then my lab manager ran past me. She was running swiftly in a great mood and asked me if I was heading home for lunch. On hearing the word "home" I burst into tears and said, "I don't have a home…"

But life had to go on. I gathered myself together again and went to find another basement apartment. At least these were relatively cheap, even though they were damp, cold, and cramped.

I soon found a place within walking distance of the IOZ building. It was two floors below ground, which made it even cheaper at 200 Yuan a month. It was a big shared room with around 16 people with the same gender. The room was big with cheap bunk beds all over. When you changed clothes or put on pajamas you turned around and pretended that no one was around, or you could hang up a cloth to shield from others if you could install some posts. It was hard to maintain privacy, nor did people care that much for 200 Yuan a month. It seemed a reasonable compromise to people who populated it. It wasn't a desirable living condition and no one went there willingly; it was done because of a lack of alternatives at difficult times.

I slept on an upper level of a bunk bed in the corner. My roommates were street vendors, illegal underage workers from other states, and dreamers who were pursuing a difficult career. People worked on different schedules, so noise was a big problem that was hard to control. There was a smelly bathroom down the hallway and men and women shared the bathroom sink area. The bathroom sinks served as our laundry place where we brought our own basins to wash clothes. Even though I disliked the living conditions, I understood that I needed to endure these ordeals to achieve my dream, so I was fine with it.

I made friends with a few of my roommates. I got to know their stories and how they ended up in the apartment. One girl who was my age was pursuing her dream to be a singer and was looking for opportunities in Beijing. I loved her deep voice for nostalgic songs and I could hum with her. Another girl told me the secret of how she faked her age in order to work in the mall and make some money for her family back home in another state. There was also a woman my mom's age who had left her husband and was trying to start her own business. I got on very well with people with diverse backgrounds and I loved learning about their stories. It fascinated me.

Regardless of their backgrounds, my new roommates all provided great emotional support for me as I followed my dream. We understood where we all came from and we encouraged each other.

I found it odd that my college friends, who were well educated, seemed to think it was strange of me to undergo painful experiences and risk everything for a dream that was unlikely to happen, while my poor bunk bed friends cheered me on enthusiastically.

My basement roommates were not people who understood the process of going abroad and the challenges involved in my journey, but they were people like me who were also pursuing their unlikely dreams. Therefore, they understood what it was like to protect your dreams, stand up to serious challenges, and to endure harsh environments for a cause that's meaningful to you deep inside. That is why paradoxically my poor underground folks cheered me on.

I was very thankful to my college friends though for trying to talk me out of pursuing an unlikely dream; I knew that they did that out of love. Had they not cared at all they would not have even uttered a single word. They tried to talk me out of painful endeavors because that was what they perceived in their mind, that I was going to suffer. Therefore, I understood why they said what they said.

People can have their own views about what was best for you, but you will have to answer your deep inner callings because you are the one living your life. Others may not see what you see and think what you think. When there is a conflict, acknowledge that they are doing what they are doing out of good intentions in their own mind. This way you are still grateful for others for giving you a different opinion. But always follow your true feelings, and be prepared to take full responsibility for your own decisions and the actions that you take.

A Shattered Dream

During my nearly 10 months' stay in IOZ, I spent most of my time inside the lab, and only went back to my apartment to sleep. I kept in touch with Jan by email, letting her know what was going on in my life and how my work was going. She always kept me updated on her travels and research too.

Time flew by fast. April 15, 2005 came around and I knew from my research that this was the deadline to receive acceptance letters from US graduate schools. I received no messages, which meant that I wasn't accepted.

My mom, who had always been one of the few who supported my dream, soon changed her tone. She said that I was wasting my time chasing a possibility that didn't exist and that I should face reality now and find a job.

I was so sad and disappointed. Could it be how this was going to end, after conquering all those difficulties? Was life playing a big joke on me?

But deep inside a different question was nagging away at me: how could things change so that it would happen? I didn't know the answer to that question, but I still had a feeling that something would change. I wondered what it would be and decided to be an observer for a while, and let fate take over.

I soon received an email from Jan explaining to me that this year the finances were very tight, so Wesleyan would not take any international students. They would only take a few US students in the biology department. But she was very kind and said that if I had any means to come to the US, she would train me. For example, if I could come with a husband, or if I was accepted by other schools that I applied to, I could transfer to her lab and she would train me. All I needed was to be physically in America.

When I read the email, my heart sank. I appreciated her offer but knew that it was impossible. I replied to her explaining that I didn't have a husband and it was impossible for me to get accepted by any other US school because Wesleyan was the only one I had applied to.

Since our interview, I knew that no other professor would be able to understand me and my story like Jan did. My scores certainly would not get me in anywhere else and, even if I did get in elsewhere, I still wanted to be at Wesleyan. It had come down to this: either Jan's lab or failure. That's why Wesleyan was the only school I applied to.

I understood the risk I had taken and now it seemed that I had failed. I had no regrets because I had tried.

But still a voice inside kept asking me how things could *change* to make it happen. I kept watching again from a distance, with no emotions attached. It seemed that the worst had happened, so there really was nothing that would worry me anymore. I was letting go completely. Deep down I felt there was a way to turn around and I wondered what would happen next. I decided to not pass any judgment but simply be an observer from a distance.

Jan was shocked to hear that Wesleyan was the only school I applied to. She didn't know that I was so dedicated to her lab, as I hadn't told her before. She said that I would have to wait another year and, during that time, build up more lab experience so I would be more prepared next year. I replied to her again and said that I appreciated her suggestion, but I felt that there was no second chance for me. Waiting another year was not an option for me, it was now or never. And it looked like I was never going abroad, so I was ready to give up. I didn't feel upset, I would simply accept the joke that life had played on me. I was taking it all in and accepting everything that had just happened.

Piecing the Dream Back Together

A few days later, I received an email out of the blue from Wesleyan Biology Department saying that things had changed and, suddenly, they had an opening for one international student. Since I was their top candidate, due to Jan's strong recommendation, I should expect an invite to an interview shortly.

I was so thrilled! I couldn't believe what was happening! Deep down in my heart, I was so grateful for the Universe. I knew that it wasn't a coincidence, that it was bound to happen. I didn't understand the *how* but I was simply being immensely thankful.

On the night of April 22, 2005, I picked up the telephone nervously inside the lab where I was working; it was a call from the other side of the globe. I heard Jan's familiar and reassuring voice, which eased my nerves. Her lab manager and a current graduate student, who was also a Chinese girl, were present too.

It was a relaxed and enjoyable chat. They asked me how my life was, how my work was going in the lab, and what I would like to do in Jan's lab. They wanted me to ask them any questions I had, so I asked about the weather and how student life was at Wesleyan.

Soon after that conversation, I received a notification letter of acceptance from Wesleyan. Finally, my dream had come true! For over a year I had been trying to get to the US and all my life I had held the dream of helping my family change our fate, and now it felt like all the suffering and hardship was totally worth it. I ended up being the only one in my class who made it to America for PhD studies in that school year, and I owe it to determination and the help from the loving Universe.

Along the way I was always determined, but sometimes felt like a candle in the wind that could be blown out at any moment. Often times, it seemed that I was drifting without touching the ground, or walking inside a dark tunnel with no end, but I kept going. I trusted the Universe and I was blessed with "miracles."

It reminds me of Mark in the movie *The Martian*. When stuck on Mars for extended time, first he thought it was the end of the world, that he would soon die. But the desire to survive kept him going, inventing ways to plant potatoes for survival. At one point during the farming process he nearly ended his life due to the unique growing conditions he had to comply with. His life was hanging on a string. Finally, a plan was made for him to connect with the crew made up of the best astronauts on Earth that were coming to rescue him. It was not an easy task though, since it takes miracles to be rescued, and the crew was risking their lives also. It was Mark's very last opportunity for survival.

To make things happen Mark built his "spaceship." He needed to jump out of his "spaceship" when the rescuing spaceship was approaching arm's length in space, provided the calculations were accurate and the spaceship traveled as predicted. One hand from the rescuing spaceship had to reach out for Mark's hand and grab him to the rescuing spaceship. If the attempt failed, Mark would disappear into the vast outer space and death would be the only result. Imagine the pressure there for Mark, and the strong desire to reach for the last string of hope to survive. He can either make it or die.

It was a captivating moment filled with excitement, uncertainties, and an enormous amount of pressure. Fortunately, the miracle did happen, and Mark was rescued and made it back to Earth. Me coming to America felt in a similar way in that I burned the ship and made it my "last" chance. I jumped out of my "spaceship" with great faith. It takes great courage and trusting and the ability to breathe through fear.

Sometimes life challenges feel like that. Perhaps in hindsight it appears that you are destined to succeed. However, when living in the moment of extreme challenges, you may not be able to see yourself making it, or chances are so slim and disappointing that giving up seems like the only option. But you just have to hang in there and push it through, and most importantly you have to have faith in yourself. If you listened to your inner callings and live to your fullest capacity to reach for your dream, it will become a reality. It may even look destined looking back, but you know how you deserved it because you did your very best and didn't give failure a chance. Reach for your dreams like it's your last chance to survive, and see what happens. I bet you will meet with miracles.

Me being accepted by an American school was the light at the end of the tunnel, and it was such a relief for me. After countless sleepless nights and painstaking endeavors, I had finally made it! It was nothing short of a miracle in my mind.

I wondered what else I could accomplish in life, if I was able to make it abroad against all odds. I realized the deep meaning of *where there is a will, there is a way.* When you have a strong will and act upon it with faith, when you have mentally eliminated the possibility of failure, the Universe will reorganize itself and make things happen. But you must do your part and act with determination and faith in yourself, despite the fear.

My parents were so excited and proud of me; and I was appreciative that they had allowed me to pursue my big dream, supporting me any way they could. Mom raised me to be honest and dad never put any constraints on what I could and could not achieve.

The day before I left China, my family had a reunion and that was the last time I saw my dad's parents. In the previous few years whenever I came home they always saved goodies for me such as fruits, but more often than not the goodies went bad by the time I arrived home because they just would not eat them. I knew how deep their love was for me. They were so old and frail, and became more sentimental than ever.

Both my dad's parents were in their early seventies, but my grandpa had lost almost all his teeth and shrank to a pile of bones, and my grandma's hair had turned pure white long ago and she faced many health issues. They were so hopeful for me though, wishing me a wonderful future. They had never imagined that their favorite granddaughter would one day be flying abroad. At the same time, they were afraid that they would never see me again. I smiled and said that they would and told them to wait for me to come back. I knew that I was just comforting them and wanted to cheer them up. I was very sad deep inside because I knew that this time it would be a long while before I could return. I was afraid that they would not last much longer and may not survive the day when I came back home again. But still I wanted to fill them with the hope that they should look forward to the day we reunite again.

On the night of August 22, 2005, I landed in Connecticut, with $200 cash in my purse, forwarded by Jan. She asked the lab manager who happened to visit China that summer to give me the money. A few clothes and the cash given by Jan were all I had in this foreign land. I became one of the four graduate students in Wesleyan biology department that school year, with the rest of the three recruited from the locals. I moved into a bright and spacious apartment on campus, with a room all to myself, a fridge, and even a kitchen. It felt unbelievably luxurious. It felt like I was in a dream. Later, Jan also secured a refund for my flight from the biology department, which I was immensely grateful for. One woman completely changed my life and turned my life around 180 degrees. I am forever indebted.

It was not only the living conditions that were beyond my expectations; I also got a handsome monthly allowance. That helped me pay off the three-thousand-dollar debt to my middle school teachers, who were kind enough to lend me money to pay off my college loans before leaving the country.

And so began a new life.

Chapter 5

Lessons in Love

真挚 *(Zhen Zhi) denotes treating every relationship with sincerity, honesty and integrity. My dating experiences have taught me a lot about relationships – and more so about myself. Always be trustworthy to others, but don't be afraid to move on if it's not what is meant to be.*

Touching Down in America—But Leaving My Heart in China

Even though my new life began in the US, my heart was left behind in China.

While I was working at IOZ, I had had my first relationship. It was so unexpected, but I fell in love uncontrollably. Jian was working in Dr. Feng's lab for his master's degree, and he was four years older than me.

He was very kind, easy going, and loved helping people. Everybody, including me, knew that he had a girlfriend from college, even though no one had seen her. Jian called his girlfriend every once in a while, since she was in another state. They had been maintaining a long-distance relationship for a few years. He told me that they met in college and, because they had had sex, they had to commit to each other. At that time, most Chinese people were still conservative, and sex meant a really big commitment. Both families expected them to get married one day. He felt a sense of responsibility to marry her when he finished school.

Jian was very selfless. He helped me do experiments, taught me new skills, and shared lunch with me sometimes. I tried to help him out as much as I could. We felt that we were kindred spirits, because he was also from a poor village family in another state.

One time, a family from his village came to visit a hospital in Beijing. The young man in the family had terminal cancer and the family tried to hide the truth from him. They planned the trip to make it seem like there wasn't much wrong with him. They wanted him to see Beijing, since he'd never visited the capital, but they didn't want him to know that he only had a couple months to live. It was heartbreaking to hear the story and Jian and I helped his folks get around the city during their visit. It was raining that day and Jian and I walked under one umbrella, like a couple to receive them. His folks thought we looked very much in love.

When you fell in love with someone in times of hardship, you were especially tied together so that you both became stronger. That's how I felt with Jian. There seemed a special bond binding us together.

Moments in Love

Every time I saw Jian I felt an electrical charge running through me, it was so powerful that it energized and rejuvenated me every time. I felt like we had known each other for a long time. We were attracted to each other like magnets. It felt so comfortable and so right to be with him. The love enveloped me; I felt addicted to this love and did not want time to pass.

Since Jian had a small allowance, he would treat me to lunch sometimes. We had lunch together every day for the few months we were together. Every night, after work, we would study in the lab until very late and then hang out in the small park above my basement apartment. There were benches in the park and it was the place for lovers to go at night.

I lay on his lap and we would stare at the stars. Looking into the deep sky, tears would suddenly start rolling down my face. He asked: "Why would you cry on such a beautiful night?" I replied: "This will be the same sky we will be staring at separately from opposite sides of the globe. We will be looking into the same sky, but we will never see each other again." He replied that I was silly to think like that and told me not to worry about the future, but to enjoy the moment.

I knew that deep down he was also aware that our relationship would not last, that we would have to fulfill our separate destinies. While I was hit with sentiments he chose to enjoy every single moment together.

On summer nights, we would run on the playground in Tsinghua University. Some of my roommate friends would exercise with us. They would get tired and gave up after a few laps, until it was just Jian and me. We would run many laps together.

I had been running regularly since high school and throughout college, so I was a good runner. Our breathing and footsteps were in sync on the track and it felt like the world had frozen into a single moment that is eternal. There was nothing else but he and I; everything else was forgotten. I felt the intertwining of our energies, too powerful and too beautiful.

I felt so refreshed after my runs with Jian but, inevitably, sadness would creep in. I felt that there would be no one else in this world who would run with me like that ever again. The thought of loss of beautiful moments like this overpowered me.

Even though I had many good times with Jian, my bouts of crying were quite frequent. I knew our beautiful relationship was not meant to last. The single act of shedding tears made me sentimental and cherished the relationship even more.

Deep down I knew that he was someone sent by the Universe at the most difficult time of my life, so that I could enjoy my time and understand what love was. He brightened my day and made the most trying moments much more bearable, and even enjoyable.

The Transient Love

I knew that our love was destined to be only transient. I had a strong sense that the time we were spending together then was the only time we would be together in this lifetime. I cherished these moments so much that I often ended up in tears.

My relationship with Jian lasted for eight months after I came to the US. But it felt like many, many years, almost like an eternity.

However, we never had sex, despite the strong attraction. I resisted it, because I knew that if I gave my first time to him, I would give up on my dream. In my mind, my first time should belong to my husband, and Jian was not the one. This relationship was just another test from the Universe to see if I could hang on to my dream of coming to America. I could feel that the Universe was asking if I really wanted what I said I wanted. No matter how much we loved each other back then, I knew that we were not meant to be together and that someone else was waiting for me somewhere in the world.

Looking back, I am grateful for a relationship that was fostering for both of us at the right time of our lives, so we could move on with more confidence. I knew that it was part of the journey, and I was happy that I didn't get off the train of life at that station. He understood too that we would not be lifelong partners, but he was happy that our lives intertwined.

Lessons in Love

Jian was meticulous and taught me many experimental skills hand-in-hand. He spent countless hours helping me improve my academic knowledge. Prior to meeting with Jian all I had were daydreams about a relationship with a man who really loved me. I was insecure and lacked confidence about my self-image. Jian always reminded me how beautiful and lovable I was, that any man who married me would be fortunate. He was never shy singing praises of me and was very serious about me boosting my self-esteem, especially in front of a man.

I learned how relationships could be so giving and trustworthy; there was nothing for me to hide. In his mind, he was willing to be a "stepping-stone" for me. He wanted to help me as much as he could on my journey to America, even if that meant that we would not be together. He presented to me a relationship full of giving without asking for returns. That was another reason why I felt so indebted to him and shed tears so often in front of him. I understood that I would not be able to repay him.

I stayed at IOZ two days before my flight to America. When he sent me off to the bus station to go home for my family reunion, I was full of sad tears seeing him going away and away and disappearing, as my bus accelerated. I knew that it was the last moment I would see this man ever again in this lifetime.

Relationships are mental. You can have sexual contact or an affair, but it could stay at the physical plane out of instinct, with no emotional attachment to the person you are with. On the other hand, your relationship can be so deep that it goes above and beyond sexual contact. It has nothing to do with the duration you are together either; some relationships you will never forget for the rest of your life because of the impact on you, no matter how transient that was. True love is above and beyond the physical plane of existence.

When you truly love someone from deep in your heart you melt emotionally with your love and would even sacrifice yourself for the other, as illustrated in many historical stories and legends. You see no boundaries and you don't expect returns, you simply enjoy the feelings of melting with each other and the total blissful state of being. You feel truly happy to serve the person you are deeply in love with.

It was only recently, after 11 years parting with Jian, that I got to understand the higher purpose of this relationship with him. From Michael Newton's books detailing soul activities in the spirit world, *Journey of Souls* and *Destiny of Souls*, I learned that before our physical birth on earth there was careful planning in the spirit world. The planning includes our life's purpose, important people we were to meet to fulfil our destiny, and of course important information concerning our relationships. I was informed by my spirit guide that when my life was planned in the spirit world before embarking on this life, there were two people who volunteered to become my husband in this life, among which was Jian. He and I shared two past lives together as husband and wife, and for this lifetime he volunteered to become my husband again.

However, there was another volunteer who I didn't have much past life experience with who volunteered to become my husband. It was set up as a challenge for my life, and my soul had accepted the challenge. It would be a significant milestone of my life to meet up and marry this man, after conquering many hardships along my journey if I lived up to it.

It was up to my free will to choose though. I could choose Jian and embark on an alternative fate. A set of completely different choices would be presented to me. It was an easier route without the struggles I had to encounter in a foreign country, however, it would mean that I would not have much personal growth as a being. The sense of inner knowing was so strong while with Jian that it prevented me from straying.

It was not easy to make decisions in relationships; you might feel overpowered by emotions. However, if you stay true to your inner being and ask the deepest part of you what you really wanted, you will find answers and therefore make the best choice at the junction. It may not seem logical or obvious on the conscious level what you should do, let your inner being guide you.

Cutting the Cord

Jian and I were deeply in love and both felt that we were inseparable, that we were becoming part of each other. Arriving in the US in 2005, I was falling to pieces emotionally because of the love I had left behind. Even though I knew that was how it would end, it was still very hard on me. I did not feel whole anymore. I felt that my energy was being depleted by not being able to see him and kiss him.

For the first eight months after I arrived, I thought about Jian every day, calling him every single night. I felt torn apart inside, and sometimes began to doubt if I had made the right decision to come to the US. But, deep down, I knew it was a learning process that I had to get over and move on from. It was a matter of time, a lot of time perhaps.

Because all I was thinking about was Jian for eight months I didn't even look at other guys or consider starting another relationship. I couldn't get him out of my mind but I couldn't be with him physically, my body felt being deprived and my heart was in pain.

Then, one day I called Jian out of loneliness. He seemed to be afraid to talk to me, and said his mom was around, and it was not convenient for him to talk. I hung up the phone feeling disappointed.

I soon received an email from a girl who called herself "another victim." I thought that, perhaps, she was Jian's girlfriend, who had found out about us. First I felt bad but then I thought that I shouldn't be worried since I didn't steal her boyfriend; I knew that they were supposed to be together.

However, the girl said that she was new in Dr. Feng's lab and Jian had started a relationship with her since I left the country. They were living together now, but she didn't know if she should stay with him or leave him. She wanted to know how I managed to forget about him and move on with my life.

This was a big shock for me. I couldn't believe what was happening. My feelings for Jian were completely ruined.

But then I thought how me leaving him must have left a heavy toll in his life. I knew how it tortured me. He must have felt the need to fill the void that was left. Seeking out a new relationship should not be considered a fault. I advised the girl that it was her own choice whether or not she wanted to stay with him, and to not feel guilty about it. I told her not to be afraid to leave either, because no one dies leaving a relationship, and time would heal everything. I wanted her to make her own decisions and understand that she could choose what feels right for her.

I decided that it was time to cut the cord with Jian. I should become a whole again and move on with my own life. Our relationship served us good purpose at the right time. I gave him a lot of assurances that he too can achieve something great and he supported me and my journey as much as he could.

My decision to follow my American dream, hence parting with Jian, was heartfelt; I followed my inner calling to make the choice. I faced the consequences of missing him and then there was the wakeup call for me. I decided that it was over. It was time for me to pick myself up and pursue a new relationship that could be out there waiting for me.

Your love stories are most likely completely different, but when you are in a relationship ask the deepest part of you if the relationship is something good for you. If it's something mutually beneficial in a deeper sense then enjoy every moment and live to the fullest, even if it is meant to be temporary. If it does not pan out, it might be for a greater good that you do not yet understand. You may find out about what the greater good is later, but stay strong and move on with your life with courage and self-confidence.

My First Date in America

Wesleyan was mostly undergraduate students. There were very few graduate students, and most men my age that I knew of were either married or not my type. My options were limited!

Lessons in Love

I was not very social, and I spent most of my time in the lab working or studying, which didn't help my chances. To "jump start" my dating life, in mid-2006, almost a year after I came to the US, I registered on one of the biggest and best dating websites. I was particularly looking for a man in science, because I thought that a female scientist should marry a guy in the same field to make the companionship work best. I liked the idea that couples help each other in their careers and share the same passions and interests. I had to open up to the American market since my seeking a Chinese guy was not successful on this and some Chinese dating websites. Apparently Chinese guys didn't hit on me.

There was one profile that caught my eye: Jack from MIT. He was in the field of neuroscience, with a background in math and computer science. I thought that he must be very smart.

I reached out to him and started a conversation. I got to know that he was not only very passionate about science; he was also in love with Asian culture. He had been to China before and loved the country. I thought that, no doubt, Jack was the one. He seemed the best match for me and we decided to meet.

At that time, I had just gotten my first car and was working towards getting a driver's license. I wanted to save money, so I bought my car for only $900 from a Chinese man who said that he was leaving the US for good. It was a 1991 Toyota Camry with a lot of mileage (179,000 miles) on it. I didn't know much about cars, but I did realize that, in the US, cars were like bikes in China. Without one, I couldn't do anything. So, I went with something cheap that could get me around.

I didn't have a driver's license yet, so I explained that to the owner. Since he couldn't find anybody else interested in his car, he decided to work out a deal with me. He helped me get a permit that allowed me to own the car legally. I wanted to make sure that I was not being taken advantage of, so I asked him to be the co-signer for my car insurance. I wanted to lock him into some sort of responsibility, so I knew that he was not tricking me.

I didn't have any family or friends in the US, nor did I have any experience in buying a car. I couldn't ask anyone for help, but I figured that a Chinese might go extra miles to help me out in this situation since he/she had had his beginning too in a foreign country, therefore he/she may understand how tough it was to get started. I reasoned there was no better person to ask than the seller.

He agreed, but warned me that I needed to get my driver's license as soon as I could. We were both taking a risk for something we thought would be mutually beneficial. I made it a goal of mine, and thought it would not be long before I had mastered driving and got my license.

I asked a new Chinese friend of mine who had been in the US for many years to sit with me in my car, while I practiced and taught myself how to drive. I wanted to save money from driving schools. I was able to ride adult bikes at the age of five and I was always good kinesthetically. Driving wasn't something I considered too hard to learn.

Now that I had made contact with Jack, who lived in Boston, there was even more reason to get my driver's license as soon as possible.

For our first meeting, Jack drove from Boston to see me in my apartment in Middletown. I was very nervous to see a handsome man in front of me, an adult American man who's looking for a date. Jack was completely foreign to me, a naive Chinese girl not yet a year in the country. I hadn't blended into the culture yet, and felt inadequately prepared, insecure, and even a little intimidated.

I had been a little reserved and introverted all my life up to that point. But in my mind, Americans were all very outgoing, talkative and social. I had very limited knowledge about foreigners at the time, and I felt so different in this foreign land. What if there were language barriers between us? What if he thought that I was not attractive or outgoing enough for him? What if the culture difference was so big that we didn't have anything to talk about?

However, Jack was very nice and understanding, and he had great knowledge about Asian countries, especially China. He had visited China a few times and had a blog about his travel. From the photos he posted, it was not hard to tell that he loved Asian people and the culture. He was awed by my bravery to come to America and pursue science, and was very fascinated by science himself. Jack sounded like someone who was eager to start a relationship. He's not the fool around type of person, nor did he have time to do so. He was very serious about his studies and spent lots of time on his graduate work. We talked nonstop for hours about family matters, interests and science, and we had good feelings about each other.

I suggested that I cook dumplings for dinner for him but realized I didn't have flour. We drove his car to the nearest grocery store but got lost on the way back since I was not familiar with the locals yet. Jack thought that it would be too late to head back to Boston if he stayed over for dinner, so he ended up driving back without dinner.

After he left I felt embarrassed. Why would I even think about cooking dinner on the first date? Why not just go out and eat? There were certainly many things I needed to improve in the romance department. Luckily, Jack didn't seem to mind my naiveté at all. He seemed so understanding and accepting; it was beyond my expectations of an American man.

A Spanner in the Works!

Jack and I decided that we should meet up again soon. He seemed to be the ideal person that I was looking for, open to Asian cultures and possessing a love of science as well as many other qualities that I loved. I was looking forward to meeting him again.

However, a few days later he emailed me and said that Boston and Connecticut were too far apart, and that he was afraid he would not have the time to meet up again because of the long drive. That wouldn't be a problem, I convinced him, because I would soon have my driver's license and could drive up every weekend to see him. I understood that he must be busy, but didn't want the distance to stop us, because I already had a great feeling about him. I was willing to do anything to make sure it would work out.

A couple weeks later I took the driving test and promptly failed! When I took my test, I was so nervous because I had loaded too much pressure onto myself. I thought about how I had to pass so that I could go visit Jack. Not only that, I had to pass so that I had a driver's license to legally drive my car, not just to own it. The pressure got to me, I made some basic errors in my test and was failed.

I found it hard to accept that I had failed my test. I stayed at the DMV window, begging them to issue me a license and refusing to leave until they did! I viewed it as a block for me to go and see Jack if I could not get my license that I considered so easy. I didn't want to give in to what I thought was fate stopping me from a possible great relationship. I would not accept the reality I was facing. I was so naïve, and I was not afraid back then in the DMV.

Then they brought the manager, who was a tall black guy with a serious look on his face. He explained to me that I needed to take the next test in a few months and there were no exceptions to this rule. I cried in front of him and said that I had to get my license because my future depended on it. I asked him to change the decision, and that I was simply too nervous and made some minor mistakes, but otherwise, I was a good driver. He smiled and said firmly that they were not going to change their decision; that I had to come back in a few months for another test.

Had I known how much power the DMV had I would not have been so persistent. On the other hand, innocent is not guilty. I would not give up unless I exhausted the possibilities that I thought existed.

I was in this new country trying to get a means of convenient transportation, but I failed the test. I did not want to be deported back to China if the policemen found out that I was driving without a license. I was afraid and didn't know what to do without passing the test. I stayed inside the DMV crying for two hours.

In the end, *I had to accept the tough reality*, and risk driving for a while longer without a license. I was very disappointed and felt bad that I was the reason hindering my relationship. In my mind, I associated passing my driving test with getting together with Jack.

I kept practicing in my old car, which could break down any time. I also went to the local driving school for some lessons without being able to pass the test.

Can you believe that, in the end, it took me seven times to pass the driver's test?! There was always something wrong: sometimes the examiner was supercritical and extra picky, sometimes I made some minor mistakes because I wasn't familiar with the road near that particular DMV. Anything that could go wrong did. It was very damaging to my self-confidence, combined with the fact that I was not able to go and see Jack as I promised him.

Despite not having a license, I still drove my friends to the grocery stores for shopping and went to Boston a couple of times for conferences, getting lost on the busy roads there. It didn't hold me back too much.

In my final driver's test, I simply let go. I had failed the previous six times. I was already used to failing by then; I was "seasoned." The worst that could happen was another failure, which I had experienced so many times it did not even hurt anymore.

With my mind being relaxed, I passed the road test with excellence, without a single error. The examiner was so surprised that my driving was so perfect. He joked that he couldn't believe why I failed my first test.

Ironically, it was at the same DMV where I failed the first time. The serious-looking black manager appeared again, congratulated me, and said "See! I knew you would pass!" He certainly remembered me, and greeted me with the biggest smile. I saw good wishes and blessings to the innocent foreigner in his eyes. He seemed so friendly and it gave me lots of warmth and encouragement. I replied "Yes, and it only took me over a year!"

So, what I thought would be a quick and easy task took a lot longer. While this was very humiliating, at least my friends got a laugh out of it. It became a standing joke, and, even for me, it's amusing now I look back on it. It was amazing how many failures I had for a task I assumed rather easy. Nevertheless, in the end there were cheers and a long-lasting memory.

Interestingly enough, the day after I got my driver's license, my car died in the middle of a busy road. A policeman appeared and demanded to see my license. I was able to proudly present it to him. What perfect timing!

When you keep failing something that you took for granted was rather simple, you get so frustrated and even start doubting yourself. It creates a downward spiral that makes the situation even worse. But if you accept the failures and are totally fine with them, then it becomes so much easier to succeed in the task.

Too often it is not that we are incompetent to accomplish the goal that we set out to do, it is that we put too much emotion into obtaining our desired results that we load ourselves with unnecessary pressure. In turn, the pressure affects our actions, consciously or subconsciously. If it ever happens to you, mentally say "So what?" and detach yourself from the outcome, you will then be able to be in the flow and let your desired result happen.

Moving On from Jack

I had been thinking about Jack all this time, holding out the hope that I could pass my driver's test next time around and go to see him. During this lengthy process of acquiring my driver's license spanning a year, it dawned on me that this relationship would never work. I was blaming myself initially for not being able to make what I thought was my ideal relationship a reality because of my failure in driving. The year that passed allowed me enough time to reflect on whether or not Jack had a real intention to be with me. I realized that if he had strong enough feelings for me, he would have driven to see me.

My thinking that if I were able to drive to see Jack, he would be pleased and love me was the problem. I had set a trap for myself, and enclosed myself within it, refusing to get out. I was my own reason for not allowing myself to move on. Through this experience, I decided not to compromise myself again to please a man.

It was not, "If I do something a man would love me." It should come naturally without me exerting too much effort trying to please the man. I should let the relationship guide me, not that I demand how things should go, same as my driving tests – that I should not strongly attach to a certain result instead of letting it flow.

I was able to mentally move on from Jack and set myself free again. I went back to the online dating service and this time decided to approach relationships with an open mind.

Soon I came across a guy named David. He looked a bit childish and goofy in his profile photo. I could tell that his picture had been cropped from a photo with his ex-girlfriend. Nobody could miss that obvious detail!

We started talking on the phone in the summer of 2007. He mentioned that he liked video games. This was such a turnoff for me, because I hated video games growing up. I had seen friends and relatives addicted to these games, wasting so much time. They would lie to parents or steal money so they could play. I thought that people who played video games lacked self-control and would have a much better future if they spent more time and energy on their studies or personal improvement.

It didn't make a good impression on me that David loved video games. On the other hand, he seemed silly, but nice. He was very blunt and said what he thought, even if it might not sound too pleasing, but he never had any bad intentions towards people. He seemed like a small-town boy.

He said that he lived with his mom, whose health was deteriorating due to terminal cancer. He had a job also, so he was working and taking care of his mom at the same time. Quite often he was overwhelmed, depressed, and stressed, and it was hard for him to cope. I felt bad for him that he had to go through this and tried to cheer him up. I wanted to help him have some hope in his life, regardless of whether the relationship would pan out or not.

My English wasn't very good at that time, especially my spoken English and my listening. David spoke quite fast, or at least it felt fast to me at the time, with occasional slang. I felt a little uncertain, and sometimes a bad phone connection made it worse. We had to say, "Pardon me?" or "What did you say?" quite frequently; it was embarrassing. In addition, David was good at using anecdotes or metaphors, which I was sure every American could understand easily, but often times it was beyond my comprehension. I could feel the "gap" between us. I was a little overwhelmed.

Still, we had quite a few phone conversations over a couple of months that summer, just to get to know each other. We never got to the point of meeting, and then one day he said that he didn't think we would be good together and we should never contact each other again and we should move on with our separate lives.

I felt a little disappointed to hear that, but at the same time I could feel the distance that we had and understood that it might not be possible for us, anyway. It was good that he respected me enough to tell me straight, and not play games. I liked his bluntness and honesty.

Our backgrounds were too different for a relationship to develop and I really couldn't imagine ever being with him. He didn't seem to be able to cope with stress, either, and lacked any ambition from what I could tell, so perhaps ending it before it began was for the best.

I was glad that David and I had some interesting chats though. Being able to talk to someone was better than being alone. I was sure that he needed someone to talk to and unload his stress. I viewed his rejection of me as his own loss, because I believed that I would have been able to help take care of his mom as well as cheer him up had we gotten together. Since I decided not to have strong emotional attachments for any outcome in a relationship, I didn't waste time to delve on it and went back on the dating service immediately. I believed that I would find a better match than David.

Lessons in Love

A Barren Dating Landscape...

Back on the dating website I soon received a "wink" from a random guy named Edward. Typically, I would not take it seriously, but I checked out his profile and decided that it might be worth talking to him. He had no photos at all on there, but his income level was well over six figures a year. I knew that he had to be a rich and successful guy who didn't want to disclose too much information.

Following my hunch, I sent Edward a message and we started a conversation. We decided that text messaging was a better way for us to communicate, so we exchanged contact information for online chatting. He asked me a lot of questions about my background and I never held anything back. He was a bit elusive about his information though. He seemed hesitant to open up. I could understand why someone important might not want to expose too much information before building up some trust, and that was fine with me.

We had never talked on the phone, it was always through texts on the internet. It didn't take long before he channeled the topic towards sex every time we talked. I told him that I had never had sex before, but that didn't discourage him. He was giving me sex education with great enthusiasm every time we communicated. I didn't mind him talking about it, but became suspicious that he didn't seem to be serious about starting a relationship. He never seemed want to meet up.

I didn't understand why he didn't want to meet me. I tried to broach the topic of relationships, but he said that he was afraid of being committed and settled, and forming a family. He was nine years older than me (already 35) but still didn't feel ready for a relationship. He was just after a fling. It could be that he felt that I was not a type for a fling so he didn't want to meet up in the first place, but he did still want someone to talk to.

I had a sense that Edward had a fear of relationships and family life, and by conversing with him I got to know that it could be due to a past traumatic relationship. I thought that perhaps I could help him overcome these challenges so he could move on with his life instead of continuing to be stuck looking for one-night stands.

We continued to talk and he started opening up more and more. I got to know that he owned two companies and was one of the top successful businessmen in Connecticut. He was also vice-president of a soccer association in New England and traveled a lot to Europe with his soccer team. He was a self-made person with a rags-to-riches story, the type of person that I admire.

I could understand that such a young man with great wealth would be cautious about sharing his information with others, especially people from a dating website. His problem was that he was too young to be that successful. Women would throw themselves at him, or trick him into marriage just to get his money. In the past, he'd had women trying to seduce him, so I could understand why he was a bit resistant about opening up to relationships, let alone marriage.

I had sympathy for him. I felt bad for him in the sense that it would be hard to tell if a woman loved him for who he was, or for his money. Whether or not he realized it, I believed that he needed someone's genuine help, and I wished that I could be the one helping him come to a better understanding of relationships and recognize trusting relationships. It was a deep part of me wanting to do a good deed where I thought I had the capability. I believed that he deserved to have someone who understood him and who would support him in his career, and build a happy family life not because of his money, but because of who he was.

I thought that, for a man like him, it was very hard to find such a woman. I thought that perhaps I could be the one. He had indeed opened up a lot more to me in the six months since I got to know him. I didn't think he shared his success stories with other women he met through online dating. The fact that he was willing to share with me some of his genuine thoughts was improvement in the relationship. However, he was still keen about talking sex but not serious about meeting up.

By March 2008 I still didn't have a real date. I was still talking with Edward and listening to his sermons about sex, even though I was bored with it.

Worse still, the Wesleyan school clinic contacted me and informed me that I needed to seek treatment for the hepatitis B virus (HBV). They were going over everyone's health profiles and recommending anyone with HBV to seek medical assistance.

Barbara, the nurse I saw at Wesleyan, was very nice. She explained to me that HBV was an STD, which I needed to be careful not to transmit to others if I plan on having sex. She seemed to be very serious about it and advised me to take precautions.

So, great! Apart from having a flat chest, I also had an STD. Since my parents were both negative for HBV, it was very likely that I contracted it because of shared and reused needles in our village clinic growing up. I never thought of its far-reaching consequences to my life until this point. I wondered how I would be able to scare guys away even more. Who would want to be with me if I revealed that I had an STD? How was I supposed to get married? Would any guy tolerate what I had?

There was Edward, talking about sex but never wanting to meet up. On the other hand, even if we did meet up he would still not be satisfied since I had an STD. I felt depressed and wanted to give up dating for good. Perhaps I was supposed to die single and just had to accept it, as fearful as that thought made me.

A Harsh Lesson to Learn...

Around that time, an old friend reappeared in my life. His name was Zhuang, and he was a Chinese teacher at a local university. Zhuang was in his 50s and I met him at a Chinese art show, just after I'd arrived in the US in 2005.

Having no ride back to Wesleyan, I asked around who could give me a ride home after the show. Luckily, I found a kind couple, Zhuang and his wife, who were willing to take me. Zhuang and his wife were my parents' age; their daughter had just started college. I was very grateful to them and we exchanged contact information, so that we could keep in touch.

In the spring of 2008, Zhuang told me that he was going back to China for a visit and asked me whether I needed anything brought back. I said a pair of goggles would be good, as I wanted to learn how to swim. When he returned from China he called me up and invited me to a restaurant to meet up. I suggested a Japanese restaurant near my campus, so I didn't need to travel very far. He seemed very kind, warm and smiley. I always knew him as a fatherly type of person.

After dinner, we got into his car. He was supposed to drive me back to campus, where I had parked my car. However, he started talking nonsense. I hadn't seen what was coming. He sighed and said that his wife was getting old and dry, and that he needed some young love. He suggested that we check into a hotel and spend some time together. I was taken totally by surprise.

I had only seen things like this happening in movies and TV shows up to that point, and I felt it was disgusting that he said that. I rejected his advances firmly, and said that I just wanted to go home. He smiled and asked if I was afraid that he was too old for me. I didn't answer, but insisted that I just wanted to go home. I was very scared but pretended to be calm. The nice guy from a moment ago seemed like a totally different person, some stranger whom I had never known in my life. I was afraid that he might take me by force. What would I do then? My heart was beating so fast I could hear my heartbeat. I was reserved and had never imagined I would be in such a situation.

Just then, his wife called on his cell phone and asked where he was and why he was not home yet. He said that he was in a meeting with some colleagues. His wife sounded suspicious and reminded him to head home soon. He sounded calm like nothing had happened when he lied to his wife about the cheating attempt. I was disappointed that men could be this disloyal in marriage.

I know that it happens in both men and women every day, and many much worse things, in many families nowadays, which is sad. Staying loyal to a relationship, or even marriage had become such a difficult thing in men and women. I always thought that people should take marriage seriously, not just about getting married but more about life after marriage.

Fortunately, after the phone call with his wife Zhuang stopped persisting and drove me back on campus. Back in my new apartment in Portland, the adjacent town to Middletown, I was so afraid from the experience. It gave me chills. I suddenly felt unprotected as a single young woman in a foreign country, a place where I had nobody to turn to.

CHAPTER 6

FINDING MR. RIGHT

缘分 *(Yuan Fen) translates to predestined relationship. It means meeting with someone in seeming serendipities, but it is destined. Indeed, there are no coincidences, especially meeting your significant other. When I felt at the end of the rope in romance, the Universe came up with a plan. This is how I eventually found my Mr. Right.*

THE "LOSERS" MEETUP

After the incident with the elderly Chinese man, I felt unsafe staying alone, and I really felt that I needed the protection of a boyfriend at my side. This time I wanted a *real* boyfriend and a *real* relationship.

I looked back on the guys I had previously contacted. Unfortunately, there didn't seem to be any one of them who really cared about me.

Even though I had been talking with Edward for over six months, it seemed he didn't ever want to meet up. Obviously, a man who didn't want to see the woman meant that there was no chemistry. There was no love, not even dating. How pathetic. I was still talking to him with the hope of changing him one day. I finally decided I needed to stop compromising myself and find myself a man who truly loves me.

David's name popped into my mind again. He was someone who was not too complicated. At least he was frank and respected me, and he seemed family oriented, which was what I needed so much.

But it would be embarrassing if I called him. He had already rejected me nearly a year ago and had probably moved on. On the other hand, he was the only one who had come close to what I needed.

I didn't know if it was a good idea to call him or not. I paced up and down in my apartment, until I finally summoned up the courage to dial his number.

I was glad that he still remembered me. After greeting each other, he asked me how my life was going and if I was dating anyone. I didn't want him to think that I was a fool, so I said that I was dating Edward, and that we had been talking to each other for over six months. David must have thought that I misunderstood talking to be dating, so he inquired a little further about how my relationship was going. I said it was going well except that Edward never seemed to want to meet up.

David said, "He's not serious; he's just playing with you. Don't talk with him anymore. He's not doing you any good." But I defended Edward, saying that I felt that he was still a good guy.

After the phone call with David, I would occasionally see him online and we would start chatting. As we opened up to each other more, my relationship with David deepened. In some way, we were both losers who couldn't find a date, and we could both laugh at dark jokes about ourselves. We actually found a lot of similarities and compatibility between us despite the huge cultural background differences. We felt like kindred spirits.

We decided to hook up and see what happened. On March 26, 2008, we met for the first time at a Thai restaurant in Middletown and had lunch together.

David was an Irish-Italian man, 27 years old when we first met. He was one year older than me. He was 5'10" and average in size. He had very fair skin and thick brown hair. He joked that he had an Irish look but Italian blood.

I already knew that his parents divorced when he was 10 years old and he and his sister lived with his mom ever since. However, both he and his sister were also very close to his dad because the dad took them out for dinners and movies all the time, and also supported them financially.

After our first meeting, David would come to visit me whenever he had a chance after work or on weekends. Seeing me was like a retreat for him, and I looked forward to seeing him every time. We held special places for each other in our hearts, and we loved each other's company.

Being a Westerner David didn't know how to use chopsticks. He practiced so hard that dinner with him would take longer than usual. It was fun to watch him in all thumbs, but I didn't think he had to go through this. I told him that it was not a big deal to just use a spoon or fork, but he insisted on mastering chopsticks. He took it very seriously and soon was able to start chopstick wars with me over the dinner table.

David was a little like my brother in the sense that he too liked to pick on me and make jokes, but in an entertaining way. He liked the fact that I was not offended by his dark jokes and he didn't need to filter himself a lot around me, for which he was very grateful. Life with him wasn't dull; he always tried to spice things up.

A First and Last Meeting

We had visited David's dad a couple times in Avon. His dad was short, and very outgoing and affectionate. He respected women and treated ladies nicely, including me. Since their family was mostly Italian they hadn't interacted with a lot of Chinese people. It was fresh for them to see me around, and I was very welcomed by David's dad. He also respected that I was a scientist obtaining my PhD degree. To him I was someone who knew what I was doing and quite smart. I loved David's dad's warmth, friendliness, and his witty humor. David was very close to his dad, and the two looked alike too.

One day in early May of 2008, David invited me to see his house in Cheshire where he lived with his mom, who was terminally ill with breast cancer. He was a good caretaker of his mom and didn't invite me to see their house until then because his mom needed her rest. He planned all his activities, including seeing me, around his mom and was never away for too long. It was a big deal to David that he invited his girlfriend to see his house and his mom.

He gave me his home address and I drove there in my new car, a white 1999 Toyota Avalon. Due to my bad sense of direction, I got lost in his neighborhood and I had to call him for directions.

David managed to guide me to his house and, when I arrived, he came out to receive me. He was standing by the door in the soft sunshine; he seemed like a tender, friendly family guy standing there, welcoming me. He was reassured that I finally found the way home. I felt warmth while wondering would he be the guy I would be returning home to everyday. I felt safe and bathed in love. This big American boy was so cordial and affectionate to me that I felt so lucky.

I met his mom, Maureen, for a few brief seconds. She was very weak and frail, and had to rest. I wished that I had known her earlier so I could have helped out. That was the only time I saw David's mom. Soon, on Memorial Day in late May 2008, she passed away.

According to his mom's will, they would sell the house and the money would be split between David and his sister, and part of it would go towards their college loans. Before the house was sold, David had it to himself and we moved in together. We would spend every night together, either there in Cheshire or occasionally in my Portland apartment until my lease ended.

Finding Mr. Right

I had long ago told David that I had hepatitis B, and luckily, he didn't seem to care about the STD part. He was vaccinated like the majority of people. What he worried about was that I might have poor health. Since he had lost his mom to cancer, he urged me to have my health checked regularly, and he was very serious about it. Not only that, he was also very serious about me getting my dental work done. Before I met him I only saw dentists when I had pain, because as a foreign student studying abroad I was still living a Chinese lifestyle and especially tried to avoid expensive dental procedures.

David almost forced me to have necessary dental surgeries done that cost about $3000, which he paid out of his own pocket. He was just a regular guy earning from an average job. I couldn't believe that he was so generous when it came to my health and well-being.

I really appreciated what he had done for me. He was not a guy putting on an act to get what he wanted. He treated me like a family member. Finally, I felt that I had a real relationship with a guy who truly cared about me, almost three years after arriving in the US.

Prior to meeting Mr. or Ms. Right, you might have lots of stories of relationships with disappointments, helplessness, or even a broken heart, but when you meet the right person you will realize that all the past challenges are part of the journey and are well worth it. They were exactly what you needed at the right time so you would meet the right person. Always think about the lessons you learned and how it propelled you forward.

Be cordial and caring in each and every relationship and stay truthful to yourself. Always have good intentions regardless of the relationship working out or not. If the relationship did not work out the way you would like, there was nothing to worry about because it could be for your higher good. Move on strongly with the knowing that there was someone else more compatible waiting for you. The Universe will bring out the right circumstances, events, and happenings to bring you and your partner together, and the way the Universe does it may be well beyond your conscious reckoning. Simply trust and let it happen.

When you find the right people in a romantic relationship it may not seem that everything would be magnificent and breathtaking; love is in the little everyday details. It could be a comfortable feeling with each other, or that you don't need to put on a face mask, or try hard to please your partner. You can simply be yourself, give love generously and be loved as well. It's a feeling that it's what is meant to be.

Pushing Through Homesickness

A few months later, I decided that now that I had a legitimate boyfriend who I could announce to the world, I would take him to China to see my family. A lot had happened back there.

My dad's parents had both died. I was very sad that I wasn't able to make it home to see them for the last time. My grandpa's health had already plummeted by the time I left China. He was always known as a strong figure with a short temper, but in his final years he was very sentimental and so frail. I did a freeform dance in front of him the day before I left the country as my way of inspiring him. I saw that his soft gaze was full of hope and joy.

Soon after I left the country, the doctors predicted that my grandpa would not survive another two months. My parents didn't give up but instead kept having him treated and telling him that if he waited another summer he would be able to see me coming back. Amazingly, my grandpa survived another whole year with the belief that he needed to stay alive to see me. Unfortunately, he died without his dream coming true. My heart was broken upon hearing the news. My grandma survived another year after my grandpa died.

Before my grandma passed away, she experienced hallucinations. She told my dad that I went home to see her with goodies and she yelled at my dad for hiding the goodies from her. When my dad told me on the phone how he corrected my grandma that I hadn't flown back to see her, I was quite upset with him. I told my dad that it didn't matter if it was a hallucination or not, as long as it appeared real in her own mind, that my dad should let it be.

My grandma seeing me was a mental event that happened to her. It was not physical, but it appeared real in her mind and it served her a good purpose. I knew that there was meaning to her so-called "hallucinations"; it was also a testimony of our special bond. She was so desperate to see me come back, and she certainly needed closure before moving on to her next existence.

If my soul has the ability to travel without time and space limitations, which I believe souls can, I would have traveled to her and let her know that I missed her so much and that I cared about her. In that sense, I was very grateful that she had her visions; it reassured her that I was with her. Did my soul indeed travel to see her? No one knew, and it didn't even matter. As long as she felt it, it was completely real to her mind.

Sometimes we brush things like this off as nonsense because the event did not appear physical to us, but physical reality is only a small part of ultimate reality. On a deeper level, there might be a meaning to perceptions that could not be explained by the physical laws. Pay attention to these types of happenings, feelings, and emotions, and seek their true meanings. The Universe is full of good intentions, you just need to be open to receive the higher truth.

I missed my home a lot during my first three years in America; I had never been away from home for so long, nor so far away from my hometown. Often times I woke up from dreams with the feeling that I was only two hours away from home and I started blaming myself for not going home for a visit, until I fully awoke and realized that I was on the other side of the globe from home. I was missing home and my family dearly, but I was determined to make my life in America work out before I could go back again.

I was so afraid of going back to the poor life that I had lived that I didn't want to go home until I had accomplished something, despite my feelings of homesickness. I was never short of motivation to do well in my studies and personal life; I was desperate to be able to go home and see my family again.

My parents had been worried about me because they thought that I was too goofy to seek out a boyfriend; I was a bookworm in their mind.

My mom had me when she was 22. I was almost 26 and she doubted I would ever find a guy. I felt that it was the perfect time to take David with me to China as proof. Plus, having never been to China before, it would be an adventure for him.

A Surprising Proposal

When I told David about the idea, he became really concerned about legal issues. He had never had much experience with foreigners and was very apprehensive about making the trip. His sister was a lawyer and they also had a family acquaintance who was an immigration lawyer.

He consulted them about whether I would be able to come back to the US if I went back to China for a visit. They both said no, very firmly. If I went back to China, they said, I would never be able to come back to the US because I only had a student visa.

I knew that it was not true at all. I would be able to come back just like the many Chinese students who I had seen travel back and forth without any issues. After a Chinese student was accepted by an American University for higher education, the student could acquire a student visa that allowed him/her to enter the US. However, this visa was valid for only one year for Chinese students, meaning if he/she went back to China after a one-year stay in the US the student would have to apply for a new visa.

The truth is applying for a new visa to reenter the US could be an issue sometimes due to the complicated procedures, but as a rule of thumb students could acquire a new student visa to complete their studies. How could a qualified immigration lawyer think otherwise? However, both lawyers strongly insisted that I would never be able to come back to the US again due to the fact that I was studying biology and stem cells, and that the Chinese government may want to keep me for themselves.

David was frightened; he didn't want to lose me. I assured him that everything was going to be fine, but he didn't trust me. He even tried to talk me out of going back to China. He wanted me to stay with him instead, but I insisted on a trip home.

The lawyers said that the only way for me to come back was if David and I got married and I obtained a green card. David truly believed that that was the case.

A couple of weeks later, to my surprise, he knelt down and proposed to me with an imaginary ring! He wanted me to marry him so I could be with him forever in the US. I was a little shocked and excited at the same time. I said yes!

We had only been seeing each other for seven months at that time, but I felt that David truly cared about me. Regardless of whether the immigration lawyer's fears were well-founded or not, the episode demonstrated to me that he was serious about me and didn't want to lose what we had. I thought that nobody else would do that for me.

Later he told me that he had hesitated before proposing to me. He wanted to make sure that he wasn't doing it simply to make sure that I could come back to the US. He contemplated how much he really loved me and how he wanted our love to last a lifetime. My incurable disease (HBV) was one of his biggest concerns. One time when listening to the radio he heard of someone who had undergone a liver transplant and recovered from HBV. He thought that was what I would need one day. He joked that he would have to be my donor.

David was also afraid that I might die much earlier than him, so he would have to risk going through the pains of finding someone else again! I knew that he was half joking about that, but the fact that he still wanted to marry me despite his perceived risks, was enough proof that he loved me deeply. That was all that mattered.

Mixed Reactions

We decided to get married as quickly as possible, and set the date for November 1. That gave us 17 days to prepare for our wedding!

David's dad agreed readily to bless the wedding. I was very surprised that it was so easy for his family to accept our rather radical plans. I had only met his dad a couple of times, but he seemed to like me. I had never even met David's sister.

Of course, my family would not be able to make it over to the wedding, but I knew that both my parents were very happy with my choice. Since they themselves had married against family wishes, they certainly wanted to give me the freedom to do what I felt best. They didn't care much about background, education, or family. As long as I was in love they would support it, and my own happiness was all what they cared about. The fact that, all of a sudden, not only did I have a boyfriend, but I was also engaged to be married in 17 days didn't faze them at all. In fact, they were all so excited for me.

Once we made the big decision, we started working on getting the engagement and wedding rings. We were both very frugal; we didn't have much money, so we borrowed some rings from David's Aunt Leslie. She kindly accompanied us to get David's ring too.

It was a really busy time. When I told my friends about my engagement and marriage coming up, I received mixed responses in the beginning. Some people around me had been dating for five years and weren't even engaged yet.

Some of them congratulated me, but others were wondering when their guys were going to propose to them. Most thought that I was so lucky to get engaged so quickly, but some thought that it was all too rushed, and that maybe we weren't taking it seriously enough. How could someone get married after knowing each other for just a few months? In addition, it was a marriage across continents with dramatically different cultural backgrounds. It seemed unbelievable in such a short period of time.

But everyone who heard about my wedding was thrilled and tried to help out as much as they could. It was like Wesleyan students and staff were my family.

One close friend warned me, and asked, "Is David really someone you want to marry?" She was concerned because she knew that I had always wanted to marry a scientist. But I said, "Yes, I think he truly loves me and I want to spend my life with him."

She congratulated me anyway, even though she wasn't sure of the relationship and thought I was perhaps taking an important life decision too lightly. I knew that she was saying that out of good intentions for me and wanted me to have a happy marriage and life in general, therefore I was very grateful to her.

In my early dating years, I wished for a scientist because I wanted someone who shared the same passions and career. As my life unfolded I realized that an ally in a career is not the determining factor, but mutual love is indispensable. When you find the right person the decision of marriage may not be that hard at all. It all seemed so natural, it's what was meant to be. Through the time we were together, David and I both felt that we were meant for each other. To the outsiders our decision to get married could seem too soon, but deep down we knew that we had found the one.

Marriage is such a big commitment that sometimes people around you want to give you their opinions and understandings. You should stand in their shoes and understand why they think the way they did. You will find that they are coming from a position of good intentions. Acknowledge their good intentions for you and be grateful to have them on your side. However, you are the one in control of your own life decisions, and you know best what is good for you. Stay true to yourself and make the final decision based on your true feelings instead of other people's opinions. You are the one who's going to live your life with your spouse for the rest of your life. At least that should be the intention at the time of the marriage.

Our Big Day

David's grandma and Aunt Leslie helped me pick out a gorgeous wedding gown and also helped me with the fitting. David's dad generously paid $700 for it. His sister was also helpful and only too happy to assist with all the wedding arrangements. I really appreciated the effort, which was made more difficult by the fact that she lived in Baltimore and had to do all the helping and planning long distance. Their mom had passed away in May and the grieving had put a lot of pressure on the family, but now they had a chance to prepare for a more joyous occasion.

The wedding itself was small but sweet. Because of the time and cost limitations, we only invited 35 family and friends, and it was held at a local restaurant. All we cared about was announcing that we were officially husband and wife.

David put lots of thought into his speech for our ceremony. It was very funny and made everyone laugh. He vowed to learn Chinese before the kids and I could make fun of him in Chinese, but apparently his mouth wrote a check his mind couldn't cash.

David picked out our wedding music. He spent a lot of time choosing and arranging the music. We would listen to each of the songs over and over and make sure that they were really what we wanted. For the majority of the songs it was my very first time hearing them, but David was really good at picking out the right music and they were so beautiful. It touched me every time hearing the songs, such as *Total Eclipse of the Heart* and *You Spin Me Right Round*. *Taking a Chance On Love* was the song he picked out for our first dance.

We didn't hire a DJ, but played the music ourselves. David used his Dad's portable home theater system to play the music. He was so paranoid about everything being perfect that he even brought two copies of every CD he made just in case one didn't work, even though he had played them in their entirety beforehand.

During our dance together, we looked into each other's eyes with love and pride. I could feel how excited David was because he couldn't stop smiling and kissing me. His eyes were fixed on me all the time with a soft and loving gaze like I was the center of this world. He couldn't stop commenting how beautiful I looked. I felt like the luckiest woman on earth, having a handsome loving husband by my side. Never had any man treated me the way he did. I saw love, compassion, and great joy in the big boy in front of me, who I called husband from that day on.

After the wedding ceremony, we went back to David's house. He was so excited to have me as his new wife. Even though we didn't take any days off work, we were happy to spend every day together as a couple.

We lived in David's house for a few months until it was ready to be sold, and, by that time, my lease in Portland had been terminated. We moved to Wesleyan campus. David worked at a software consulting company, while I was still finishing graduate school.

Our wedding was well timed, because I was writing my first paper, my first publication, so I was able to use "Xu Maisano" as my author name.

When we moved to Wesleyan we lived a very happy life. We planted a garden in the backyard and grew some vegetables. It was not as much about the produce but about the process that we enjoyed together. We led a simple, carefree life.

David had been so depressed with his mom dying so young, but now he had a sympathetic ear and someone to talk to, and I had someone to lean on as well. We were very happy to be together and it felt like we were getting stronger every day, moving ahead with courage, trust, and love.

The essence of a wedding is to formally, publicly, and legally announce to the world that the two of you have become one. That your love for each other is so strong and unending that you want to codify the relationship and vow to be together in sickness and in health until death parts you. It is embarking on a new journey because of your love. The ceremony is a ritual expression of an indefinable bond and strong commitment between the two of you, and the superficial things do not matter.

Other things equal, such as baptisms, funerals, swearing an oath of citizenship, graduations, signing a mortgage, or whatever you go through in life, make the decision to focus on the core meanings instead of the bells and whistles (clothes, food, transportation, music, or display of splendor). You will find that keeping the deeper meanings of societal rituals in the forefront of your mind elevates your consciousness and enables you to enjoy your special moment to the fullest in a way you would like it to be.

Back in China Again

The following year, in the summer of 2009, I got my green card and we were finally able to travel together. By the time we decided to travel, I was already two months pregnant with our first child, but I was not showing at the time.

David wanted to have a more carefree time together and let me be the center of his world, but I was keen to start a family. I felt that we were ready to have a child. Even though he wasn't quite sure, I felt that it would be fun and make our life even happier and our relationship even closer.

He soon agreed. I think he would have done anything to satisfy me. I was pregnant by the time we flew to China. I hadn't been home since arriving in the US, so it had already been four years since I had seen my parents. David said that I would cry on seeing my parents, but I insisted, "No, that's not going to happen."

David took out his camera, ready to capture what he believed would be my moment of weakness and prove his point. I shook my head and laughed at how serious he was about his bet.

When we came out of the airport and I saw my parents there leaning on the bars, waiting for me, I saw how intense and focused their eyes were as they searched for me in the crowd. I thought how much older they looked than when I left, and they didn't seem as strong as I had always remembered them. So much seemed to have changed and I felt that they looked so vulnerable. It was such a long time since I had seen them last that it almost felt unbearable. Now the moment had finally arrived.

And David was, of course, right. I broke down, and tears started streaming down my face. I couldn't contain myself and turned my head away from my parents, trying to hide my tears. But my mom started crying too, pulling me towards her like a mother duck that had found her lost baby duckling.

David filmed it all. I wondered whether he just wanted to tease me with it, but I later found out he just wanted to capture the moment so we could keep it forever, and he wasn't really expecting me to react how I did.

After I obtained my green card, my husband, David, and I visited China in the summer of 2009. This photo was taken on the Great Wall of China with my parents.

We had a great visit and my family finally got to meet David, my new husband. Even though they couldn't communicate with each other well, everything seemed to be perfect and very joyous. My family celebrated me coming back as a holiday, and my brother took the days off from work and drove me around places.

It was interesting to see how David stood out in my small village, as no foreigners had visited before. It was quite a scene to see him having breakfast with me at food stands in my village. Some people would stare at him while passing by on their bikes and even turned their heads to look at him far into the distance. David didn't quite like the amount of attention he got from strangers, but it was a culture shock to my villagers as much as to David.

It was a very memorable visit, even though it only lasted 14 days since we didn't want to miss too much work. We visited the Great Wall, and many other attractions around Beijing. We still considered it our honeymoon.

The Healing Journey

Four years after I left China all alone, I returned home with a foreign husband and a two-months baby in my belly. The change seemed unbelievable to my folks, but I understood how much I had gone through. I didn't take for granted what I had gotten, and I understood that it was only the beginning of a new journey.

Chapter 7

Balancing Work and Family

自问 *(Zi Wen) means ask oneself and examine one's conscience. It is very important to look beyond everyday struggles and examine yourself and evaluate whether or not you are on your true path. Amidst our blessings with beautiful children and the challenges of balancing work and family, through self-questioning I realized that I was not on the right path of fulfilling my life's purpose...*

A Joyful New Arrival

After our trip to China, we returned to our place on campus and started preparing for the arrival of our first child.

My pregnancy went smoothly and every step along the way my husband took photos of my belly, caressing it, and kissing it with love. David was heavily involved in my pregnancy and he was so thrilled every step of the way. It was a very precious time in our lives.

I planned to work in the lab right up until labor so that I could graduate soon after baby's arrival. I wanted to seize every moment I could for work before life got too hectic.

As the time got closer, I was able to bring my parents to the US for a year's stay to help us out. We moved to a bigger house on campus to make enough room for everyone.

Our baby was due on March 5, 2010. But on February 27, my husband and I were in bed trying to get to sleep, and at around 11 PM, my water broke!

We were very shocked and excited at the same time. Our baby was coming! We called the doctor, who said that it was fine to stay home for a while longer, but we were so apprehensive that we decided to head to the hospital.

At the hospital, I was pacing up and down the hallway the whole night with excruciating belly pains. My husband walked with me, holding my arms. We had attended a Lamaze class beforehand, so he knew how to help me ease the pain, with deep breathing exercises and emotional support. He placed his hands under my armpits and let me lean on him for deep breathing. I also tried a hot shower, but it didn't relieve the pain much at all.

I wasn't afraid because I knew that the pain was natural. At the end of the pain there would be a huge reward. The nurses offered pain relief many times, but I refused. I had no pain medication or an epidural. I wanted an all-natural birth.

We heard some women screaming across the hallway and knew that I was headed for the same experience. But I was prepared for it and willed it to come quickly, as I knew that afterwards would come great joy, because our child would arrive in this world. We already knew that it would be a baby girl, and we named her Amanda.

I barely slept at all that night, and neither did David. At around two o'clock the following afternoon, my pain intensified, and I felt the urge to push. I asked the doctor to check on me, but they said that I wasn't in much pain judging by my response (I wasn't screaming), and that I should wait a little longer. I insisted, and they were surprised to find out that I was 10 centimeters dilated, so the delivery team quickly got ready.

David always joked that I did not show signs of pains during labor and that I had to beg the doctor to confirm that I was fully ready to push. He had fun telling the stories to other women whenever he had a chance. It was very lovely that David was full of excitement in sharing our labor stories.

I was given directions to push. It felt so close, but it was so hard, being my first labor. My husband stood by my side all the time, letting me squeeze his arms to release my pain and encouraging me to push harder so we could finally meet our daughter. He was so eager to meet our new baby girl.

After half an hour's push Amanda finally arrived in this world. The doctors were shocked by how big she was. I had only gained 27 pounds in total on top of my 95-pound frame during my pregnancy. My OB doctor had already warned me that I might have a very small baby, perhaps 5 or 6 pounds. But when she was born, our daughter was 7 pounds and 14 ounces. The doctors let out an audible "Woah!" It became one of my husband's favorite parts of the labor experience.

David was allowed to cut the umbilical cord, and then they handed the baby to me. It was surreal to hold her in my arms even though I had felt the kicks inside my belly before. If you are a parent, you know how amazing it is to finally meet the new person that is the expression of your love. You two had created that life, and you would do anything for that baby.

Amanda looked so tiny to me, despite being a surprisingly big baby. The doctors were shocked by how much hair she had. It took them a while to clean her up and brush all that hair. It was David's pleasure to watch the nurses washing Amanda's unusually thick and beautiful reddish hair that had blonde tips.

My husband couldn't stop smiling at our new baby girl Amanda, and he was so proud of me for going with an all-natural labor.

During our two-day hospital stay, he spent most of the time with me and our new baby, only going home occasionally to get things ready for our return home. Despite being busy and having a serious lack of sleep, I never saw him so excited in his life, and love was flowing from his eyes. I heard the unspoken promise of a father to his newborn child, to look after her and protect her forever.

David said how, after becoming a father for the first time, he could understand why parents would even kill for their children. The sense of responsibility and love was overwhelming. I was so captivated to see the fatherly side of him, and it reassured me that he would be a great father to our new child.

There is nothing like becoming a parent to teach you what unconditional love is. Upon becoming a parent, some people may change completely, with a deeper understanding and love towards others beyond just their own child. The miracle of bringing a new life into this world can change a person in profound ways.

You bring the little being into this world and you spare nothing to protect her and love her. There is no requirement for you to give out this everlasting love. She does not need to play cute or try to do anything to gain your favor, for loving her makes you happy and more complete. Love builds trust. With the nurture of this unconditional love, the baby loves you and trusts you completely.

Similarly, we are all children by the Universe. As we stray away from infancy, as we grow up, we forget that once we were a little innocent baby (deep inside we still are), and that we were loved unconditionally not only by our parents, but also the Universe. The Universe is what makes everything happen. Being unconditional, this love has never changed and will never change. We are loved unconditionally by the

Universe, as true now as when we were created initially. As children bathed in this love, we should love and trust the Universe completely.

A Little Star on Campus

So, from February 28, 2010, there were three of us, plus the extended family. Amanda created a lot of joy and laughter. She was the first grandchild on both sides, so she was a huge source of excitement. And she was so incredibly cute. She had a somewhat Asian face but Irish skin and reddish hair.

It was a very blissful period in our lives. I took maternity leave for three weeks, but quickly returned to work. Life was a lot more hectic with a new baby, of course, but my parents helped immensely with babysitting Amanda.

The spring came soon and, in the summer, Amanda was able to go outside a lot. My parents would stroll on campus with her. She was a very outgoing baby, and loved everything she saw.

Because Wesleyan was mostly young undergraduate students, there were few babies on campus. The students loved seeing Amanda because she was always smiling and waving at people. Even the cleaning lady on campus became good friends with her. Every time she saw Amanda she would stop and play with her. Amanda gave joy to anyone who saw her.

Sometimes the students could hear Amanda baby talking outside the classrooms, and they all loved her, even though most didn't know who the mommy was. Amanda was far better known than I was, and she became quite a little celebrity on the small campus.

Sometimes I would take walks with her on campus and lay her down on the grass to play with her. When my husband came home from work he would be immediately relieved from the pressure from work, and play with Amanda. She had the ability to cheer anyone up instantly and our lives were so much merrier with this little being around.

Recognition for My Studies

My studies were close to a completion when I had Amanda. I was finally able to defend my thesis in January 2011, almost five and a half years after I came to the US. I had put so much effort into it because I wanted to proceed to the next stage of my life without any obstacles, and this meant working extremely hard to balance work and family life.

But I was no stranger to working on weekends or taking quick lunches. After Amanda arrived, I balanced this with pumping milk in a private room before returning to work quickly.

It certainly paid off though. When I received my diploma, I had three publications resulting from my PhD study, and my main research paper was published in a well-known science journal. I was among the first to graduate in my department among graduate students of my year while I was the only foreigner.

Being eight months pregnant with Amanda didn't stop me from conducting scientific studies at Wesleyan University, winter of 2009.

My work was focused on the use of stem cell transplant for controlling neurological disorders, and was quite unique. I faced great challenges to incorporate multiple areas of expertise such as neural development, stem cell research, animal microsurgery, and electrophysiology. Each of these areas could be a stand-alone study. Because of the spectrum of techniques my project involved, it was a collaborative study among three labs at Wesleyan. I worked in an additional two labs besides Jan's. I had to learn everything from scratch, gain the knowledge, and master the techniques to make the experiments flow.

The duration of the experiments was relatively lengthy, lasting a few months, so even if one thing failed in the process I needed to repeat from the very beginning. I spent endless hours in the lab troubleshooting with lab mates, and meeting with advisers. At times it was frustrating to see little to no progress, but I never gave up, persisting even when I could not see light at end of the tunnel.

My academic achievements earned me the Barry Kiefer Prize, which is a Wesleyan University award for outstanding graduate students.

Sometimes a person's life can be changed completely because of another person; such was the case with me. Jan was the one who not only made my US dream come true despite the ordeals, but she also trained me to be a meticulous, compassionate, and tough woman scientist who never gave up on challenging projects.

Upon my arrival in the US she gave me belongings, including a bicycle, clothes and cookware, to start my new life in the US. Scientifically she was always there pushing me over my own limitations, and many times I could feel her tough love. Jan helped me come out of my own shell, which I felt because of the environment in which I was raised. I was very humble but sometimes I lacked the ability to speak out boldly about my ideas and findings, and it manifested as lack of self-confidence. Jan was great at spotting my weaknesses and reminding me of the necessary changes. Without her guidance, I would not have been able to finish my PhD study in a short five and a half years, grow rapidly professionally and personally, and balance work and family.

My graduation reception with Jan Naegele and baby Amanda on Wesleyan campus, May 2011.

I am grateful for her deep understanding and the support of other women scientists, and I am a beneficiary of her kindness. I am forever grateful for this woman who helped me turn my life around.

There are many other Wesleyan professors, staff, and students to whom I was indebted, especially professors Laura Grabel and Gloster Aaron, whose labs I also worked at. I was treated as their student, and they gave me incredible technical as well as emotional support. They helped shape me to be a fearless scientist and aspirational individual.

I always loved how close the graduate student-adviser relationships were at Wesleyan. I was especially lucky to have taken on a very challenging project that allowed me to be under the mentorship of three amazing professors.

Sometimes I was amazed by my achievement and personal growth at graduate school, but I fully understood that the reason I was able to accomplish what I did was because I was standing on the shoulders of giants. It was the important people in my life who made it possible for me. They lifted me up to new heights that I did not know existed before. They widened my horizons and expanded my vision and gave me the confidence that I could accomplish amazing things. I was always curious and thirsty for knowledge, and I was provided with the fostering environment and guidance from the Wesleyan community, including the amazing undergraduate students.

To me, pursuing a higher education is more about overcoming your limitations by taking on a demanding project seriously until you accomplish the task. It is not as much about the diploma, and you may not even work in the exact same field in the future, but it is a process that expands your existing skills and it tests your abilities. It is a serious proving ground that makes you grow.

When you experience a great undertaking, you will realize that you are not doing it alone. Seek out guidance from those who can lift you up, such as someone who has genuine interest for your betterment. Be friends with them and appreciate their help because without them you may not get anywhere. Remember that in whatever you do, people are the most important element. The situations might be difficult, but with the help of the right people you can move mountains, just as I was able to make it to the US and complete an advanced education with notable achievements in short years' span.

Big Changes

My parents soon had to go back to China because their visas were about to expire. By May 2011, I had already found a job working as a postdoctoral fellow at the UCONN health center. My new work involved studying the mechanisms of neurological disorders with neural stem cells in culture dishes.

We were able to move off the Wesleyan campus and into a beautiful apartment in Cheshire. It belonged to my father-in-law, so we were able to save money on rent. David also worked part-time for his dad when he had spare time, which helped.

At my new lab, my boss, Mr. Li, was a very pleasant and intelligent Chinese man. His wife worked as technical support in the lab too. They were both very kind and I got on well with everyone there. Everyone worked so hard in the lab, including Mr. Li and his wife. They were always there from very early in the morning until late, and it was rare to not see them in the lab on weekends. I was among a group of dedicated scientists.

I learned many new skills in the lab. Mr. Li was a very strategic, critical thinker, and was very sharp scientifically. Even though he was very strict to students and had high expectations, for some reason he was very proud of me and treated me as a friend. Work as a postdoctoral fellow was much more independent than as a PhD student, and there was more pressure to publish papers and climb up the academic ladder to professorship.

At this time, the US government was cutting down on funding for research and it was becoming harder to progress after obtaining a PhD. I heard that, when Mr. Li applied for the position at UCONN, over 200 candidates applied and competed for the same position. The competition was fierce. It was becoming common for postdoctoral fellows to work many years without progressing to the next stage of professorship or entering a pharmaceutical company. The options became limited when you climbed that high in academia.

I began to question whether or not I was heading in the right direction. I felt like I was walking through an endless tunnel every day; I couldn't see where it ended. The salary as a postdoc fellow was low. It was considered a temporary position before professorship. But I had seen so many people stuck in this "temporary" position unable to move on with their lives. Even if I moved on, what I foresaw was tedious repetition of experiments with little family time.

I could live with that if what I was doing made me feel that I was helping humanity. But I felt a disconnection somewhere. My goal was to understand the human brain and help treat neurological disorders, but experiments on cells could not address conditions in a human body. The growth of cultured cells was greatly influenced by the environment, the element in the culture media as well as the air. That was why there were so many variations and experiments were hard to replicate completely. I was puzzled.

In cultured cells, the culture condition does not mimic what happens in the human body. The internal environment of a human body, hence each cell inside the body, is much more complex. Therefore, to truly heal, one cannot dissect out a part and pretend the mind is not involved. Consciousness is involved in healing.

I did not think that what I was doing was on the right track for me. I felt the disconnection, even though I hadn't figured out yet what I should be doing instead.

If you ever feel you are "stuck" at a job, examine your inner feelings of why you feel the way you do. Of course, we all need to make a living and generate income, but first peel off the money issue and ask yourself honestly if you are passionate about what you are doing and why you are working at your job. You may not be able to take immediate actions to change your situation or quit your job, but understand that your true feelings will help guide you towards making the right decisions and finding your true path.

A New Arrival Saves My Gallbladder

We put Amanda in daycare while David and I worked hard at our jobs. I was experiencing stress at work and seasonal spring allergies, and my body started to grow weak.

I had some episodes of cramping and excruciating pains that seemed to come from the gallbladder. This worsened my feelings of stress and depression, which also worsened the gallbladder pain, particularly one night that I remember.

I went to work the following day, despite feeling weak. I couldn't miss any work. That afternoon I was in excruciating pain and I actually thought I was dying. My coworkers took me to the emergency department at the hospital on campus, not far from our lab.

However, the nurses told me that they didn't have any room available, and that I would have to wait. I doubled over on the floor in pain in the waiting room and waited, and waited. The pain was so bad that I thought I would die right there in the waiting room.

I had never felt so much pain. It was not like labor pain, which I knew was safe. This felt like killer pain, so I was overcome by fear. Eventually they came and wheeled me in and finally I was on a hospital bed. By that time the pain had largely subsided, but the doctor confirmed that it was gallbladder pain, and that I should have surgery when I got physically stronger. They recommended a doctor for me to see. I wasn't going to wait around for that pain to come again.

A few days later, I went to see the recommended doctor at his clinic. I waited and waited; the receptionist told me that the doctor was busy dealing with some emergencies in the hospital and would be back soon. I waited for two hours and he never showed up, so I walked out disappointed. I admit that I was not a good patient.

When David heard about this, he was upset and said that I should have waited for the doctor, no matter how long. He really wanted me to have the surgery to prevent any future episodes, but I somehow started to feel that it was stress-related, and should be manageable. I knew that it was because of my mindset towards my job that put me under stress. It was my body's "interpretation" of how things were going, and the pain was a reminder of misalignment. But David was so concerned that he insisted on going with me to the doctor's the next time.

We scheduled a new appointment to see the same doctor, but again he didn't show up for over two hours. I insisted on walking out again. David and I decided to look up another specialist instead.

We had already bought tickets to go to China for a second visit in three weeks' time, so it was important to get my health taken care of before our trip.

I went to see the specialist, who was very kind and knowledgeable, and he explained everything about the surgery, and eased my fears.

He convinced me that it was standard surgery and that the technology was so advanced that I should have no worries at all. I decided to have the operation within two days, so I'd be fully recovered before my trip.

The nurse helped me with a routine, pre-surgery blood test, and I was sure that I would be good to go for surgery.

One day later, I received a phone call from the nurse, which I thought was going to confirm the surgery. Instead, she said that the blood test had come back with a positive pregnancy test!

I was so stunned! As the nurse delivered the news in a monotone, emotionless voice, I was speechless, yet boiling inside. I was excited and worried at the same time, because I didn't know if my body was strong enough to carry a baby and whether it meant that I couldn't have surgery.

I told David and he had mixed feelings too. He didn't want to have a second baby so soon, though he later came to accept it.

I went to see the specialist again and he presented a couple of choices. I could wait a couple of months (before the baby got too big) to have the surgery. The recovery would still be quick and I wouldn't need to worry about having an attack during pregnancy. Or I could delay the surgery until after the baby was born. But if the pains came back during pregnancy, it was not going to be easy to manage.

I thought about how precious this baby was. It felt like it was trying to stop me from having surgery. I had been to the first doctor twice without being able to see him, then I had been determined to have the surgery done only to be stopped by this baby. It felt like this was what was meant to happen, that I was meant to have this baby and not the gallbladder surgery.

Becoming pregnant under these unique circumstances calmed me down. I realized that I was racing so hard trying to accomplish in academia that I was overcome by stress. I lost sight of my own powers. However, a new baby decided to come my way and it made me realize that I needed to think positively and stay well instead of stuck in self-inflicted stress, for the sake of the baby at least. Deep down, surgery was not what I thought the solution was. Upon knowing that I was pregnant it became clear that I needed to adjust my mindset to resolve the stress.

It was also amazing how the Universe timed things to happen. If the first doctor were there as he was supposed to be, I would have opted for surgery. The two failed visits postponed the timing for seeing the second doctor, with whom I was determined to undergo gallbladder surgery. By then, a new life was on the way that finally had me realize how I should make choices in this critical time.

Sometimes when you are under stress it feels so right to be stressful, it seems that there is no other way to feel the situation other than being stressed. There seems to be no way out and you feel stuck. Then something radical happens, perhaps a serious health issue or something unbelievable as a wakeup call, and you realize that you had been giving your power away to perceived stress and that's why you strayed away from health. With this realization, you seek to change your thinking patterns and therefore regain your power.

Sometimes you are awed by how the messages are conveyed to you. The Universe is brilliant in creating the right circumstances for your life at the right time to teach you valuable lessons. Allow yourself to be amazed during such moments and be grateful for the invisible help.

Another Beautiful Girl!

We followed our plan to visit China in the fall of 2011, when Amanda was a year and a half, and I was already two months pregnant with our second baby.

Luckily my gallbladder was fine during the trip and I had no attacks. We attended my brother's wedding and had lots of fun with my family.

However, during that trip my family became very concerned about me because I was so thin from working so hard. I was looking after Amanda, working a full-time job, *and* pregnant with my second child. My extended family insisted that one of my parents should come to America to help me out. Since my parents' travel visa would not allow them to stay long enough, we decided to let my parents take turns to come to the US. We figured that my dad should come soon, and then when his allowed six months' stay ended, my mom should come afterwards. We had to rotate my parents in those years. So, soon after our two-week stay in China, we brought my dad to the US to live with us.

My second pregnancy went amazingly well, with no gallbladder pains during the whole term. Amanda had been delivered six days before the due date, and our second child was expected two weeks ahead of schedule. I was spending so much time at work that I felt so tired all the time, and I really wanted the pregnancy to be over sooner rather than later.

But, instead, our second girl named Maureen (after David's mom) latched onto me and wouldn't let go! I told David that if she didn't come naturally by the day before the due date of May 18, 2012, I wanted to be induced.

The night before the planned induction at the hospital, around nine o'clock, I started to have contractions and went into natural labor. I was amazed by how the body works, and how perfect the timing was. Had I not started contractions I would have been induced in a few hours. David joked that Maureen must have overhead the ultimatum and decided it was time to come.

The second pregnancy and labor went smoothly. I was blessed that Maureen served as a wakeup call and prevented me from going through an unnecessary surgery. With this being inside of me it gave me a lot of strength to look at the bright side of things. I felt grateful for how things panned out and I knew that it was what meant to be.

David was by my side again for the labor and he was my biggest cheerleader. He was such a proud father and husband. We felt very blessed and excited to have another daughter entrusted to us.

Soon after Maureen was born, in September 2012, I became a naturalized US citizen. I decided to change my first name from "Xu" to "Sue" because people were getting confused. One time on the phone I spelled out my name "X, U" and the person replied "F, U!" and he hung up in anger! I was disappointed by people's bad assumptions of other people. At the same time, I realized that I needed an Americanized first name that was somewhat close to my original pronunciation to avoid future misunderstandings.

So, after starting out as Xu Liu in 1982, I became Xu Maisano upon marriage in 2008, and then Sue Maisano in 2012 upon becoming a US citizen.

Finding Life's Purpose

With a growing family and work pressures, my stress levels mounted. I found it difficult to balance everything and I felt drained all the time. I would drag my whole family to work on weekends because the kids wanted mommy. David would watch the children in the hallway while I did experiments in the lab and checked on everybody occasionally.

On the other hand, financial stresses were somewhat relieved. I was working for the state with great benefits. For example, the labor fee we had to pay when Maureen was born was only $10, instead of the thousands we had to pay for Amanda's birth, when I didn't have good health insurance. It was not hard to see why some people in the US work for health benefits. Even though my salary was quite low (less than $40,000 a year), I liked the security that came with the job.

But the stress was making me sick for seemingly no reason, and manifested as weird allergies. Suddenly I would start sneezing non-stop, get a cold that just wouldn't budge, have a runny nose, or have itchy rashes all over my body. There was always something.

These all made me depressed and I knew my immune system was compromised. I was hanging onto a job just to make ends meet, but I felt that I was going down the wrong path. I was not fulfilled, and felt more and more out of alignment with myself because of the work that I was doing.

I started to have doubts about the direction I was taking in my career, like I had steered away from my life's purpose.

I looked at my entire life, how I got to where I was, and started thinking about all the driving forces for my choices. How was I able to accomplish the things that seemed so impossible when I was growing up?

How was I able to get into the college that seemed out of reach for me?

How did I manage to get to the US when the chances were slim to none?

How had I met my husband and embarked on our lifetime journey together?

I thought about how I had met countless challenges on my journey and that it was nothing short of a miracle that I was able to accomplish what I had.

But what was my life all about? Why and how had I come across all the situations, events, and people in my life? Beyond that, what was the purpose of my life? How can I help others in need?

It's powerful when you sit back, look at your life, and search for meaning, because you nearly always find it.

As for me, I had always been trying to inspire others and help them overcome illness and self-limitations. As a teenager, I had to demonstrate to my mom that life was worth living, so that she had the courage to carry on. I always knew that I was the only one who could change my own fate, and I reached out to my dreams like it was the only way for me to survive. I didn't entertain the idea of failure when I tried to come to America, even though my chances were slim. The deep-rooted reason why I studied neuroscience was to understand why my mom got so seriously sick when I was young. I wanted to understand what makes people healthy, happy, and fulfilled. To find the answers I must first heal and empower myself, and it was exactly what my journey was about.

I saw a meaning in everything and felt that it was not just a random set of events that had brought me to where I was in my life.

My childhood experiences were big lessons for me and they shaped my awareness towards healing the sick and empowering the weak. Now, as a postdoctoral fellow, I was studying neurological disorders and trying to understand disease mechanisms. But I realized that it was all focused upon disease, not healing.

I was looking at cultured cells for answers, but human beings are far more complicated than that. For the cultured cells in a dish, the environment they were in was instrumental in regulating the singling within the cells and genes that turned on or off. The elements in the culture media, the interaction with other cells, and conditions such as the temperature and surrounding air all determine the fate and function of the cell. On the other hand, the cells within the body are also controlled largely by their environment, which is much more complicated than a dish. What is the environment for the cells within the body? How is the environment determined? What causes it to change or result in disease?

The environment within the body is "translated" from outside the body. The human body is like a perfect incubator, and body fluids are the culture media. Ultimately, the body "interprets" the outside environment through the mind by way of thinking, feelings, and emotions. What eventually becomes the "environment" for a bodily cell is the result of the interpretation of outside environments, meaning what the mind makes sense of and creates the internal environment for each cell. It is the translation of the outside environment that generates the environment within the body. To the same physical environment, life events, or situations, different people have different translations, creating different internal environment for their cells within the body. Cells then faithfully turn on singling and genes according to this internalized environment. It is the meaning we give that counts, and each person is unique in his or her perceptions. In essence, the state of the mind is involved in happiness, health and success.

Health and success are alike; they are manifestations to what we give meaning to in different areas of our life. What I was doing in my career was not really answering my questions of how I could help other people truly be healed and empowered. I realized that I had the right intentions in life but I was not following a true path I was seeking.

I realized that the path I was seeking was healing and empowerment through the power of the mind.

Chapter 8

Finding The Path

无为 *(Wu Wei), like water flowing with its yielding nature, means action without action. It means trust the perfection in the life design and act in sync with no resistance or fight, but simply flow forward in the passage, effortlessly. As my life unfolded, after all the challenges I experienced, including those in my marriage, I came to the understanding that it was perfect all along and all I needed to do was to surrender.*

A New Direction in the Subconscious Mind

I began to look for answers, trying to attune myself to my core being and accomplish my higher goals, while also balancing my family life.

I started to read self-help books like Tony Robbins' *Awaken the Giant Within* and Napoleon Hill's *Think and Grow Rich*, among many others. Tony Robbins mentioned that the reason he could help people change rather quickly was because he used hypnosis skills.

That was the first time I had heard of hypnosis. I then learned all about it and it resonated with me deeply. I was moved by Milton Erickson's legendary life stories. Milton became the founding president of the American Society for Clinical Hypnosis and was one of the most important figures in the history of hypnosis.

At age 17, Milton contracted polio and was severely paralyzed. One night his condition became so critical that the doctor predicted that he would die before the next morning. Lying on his deathbed, he asked his mother to rearrange the mirror so that he would be able to see the sun when it rose the next morning, which would prove that the doctor was wrong and that he could live on. His will was so strong that his subconscious mind blocked out the tree outside his window that would have blocked the sun. All he saw was a sunset covering the entire sky. He immediately passed out for three days, but he survived. He saved his own life with autohypnosis. He then began to recall and concentrate on "body memories" of his body's muscular activity and regained partial control of his body through training his mind. Next, he took an unassisted thousand-mile canoe trip to retrain his body and, at the end of the trip he could walk with a cane. He became arguably *the* most influential hypnotist in America in the twentieth century, helping others heal with the power of their subconscious mind.

I was drawn to Milton's story because it demonstrated the unbelievable power of the mind. He could not have seen the sun in the mirror since the trees would have blocked it, but he saw the sun in his mind and that's what mattered. The physical reality was not all there was, but it was the reality in the mind that mattered most. It was belief that saved Milton's life. It showed me the overwhelming power of the subconscious mind when beneficial belief was employed. It is also in line with what I had realized earlier, that the interpretation of physical reality/environment, not the physical reality itself, creates the inner reality/environment for the body, which is then faithfully manifested.

What is important is the meaning you give to life's happenings, and you can choose to create a reality in your mind that supports your well-being and higher purpose and therefore change your life. You determine your own life!

I suddenly understood why I was able to achieve what had seemed like impossible things earlier in my life. It was the belief that I could do it! "Reality" is not the ultimate determining factor in your life, but what your perception of that reality is in your own mind. By changing your subconscious mind, you change your life no matter where you are right now. Healing and personal empowerment are easily obtainable when you tap into the power of the mind. Unfortunately, many people do not realize the power of choice that they have but run through life as a "victim." I realized that I had been using this power unconsciously in the past, and I had been questing how I can help others the most powerful way.

I had finally found the answer to my life's purpose. I found truth and wisdom in hypnosis, and the power to change people's mind and therefore empower lives. It was clear that hypnosis was what I wanted to pursue instead of the science research I was doing. I no longer wanted to be stuck at a job and not follow my path. I was empowered to make my next big move in life, like the many challenges I had taken earlier in life. I decided to quit my job and master hypnosis.

Unsurprisingly, this was not a popular decision with David, who would have preferred that I stay in my job so I could maintain a steady income and benefits for our family. We had also just bought a new house in Southington and had a mortgage to pay, and day care fees to cover, among other expenses.

My boss had great faith in me too. He felt that I could make a great researcher and become a well-accomplished scientist.

I had to balance these expectations of me with my inner calling. I knew that I was the only one who could change myself and my situation, I was no stranger to that feeling and again I took a leap of faith and decided to pursue my dream, like I had done so many times in the past.

This time, however, it was different. I was not alone anymore; the stakes were higher. I was not only jeopardizing my own life but my family's too. I totally understood the risks involved, like many times before in my life. But I felt the strong inner calling to the point that I felt guilty trading my time for money instead of following my true passions. I did not believe making this move would hurt my family; instead it was a long-term vision that would benefit my family and many others.

With my kids growing I wanted to be around them more often, and quitting my job and becoming a healer would allow me to spend more time with my children compared to my science job, despite the short-term difficulty of establishing a new career. By embarking on a healing path that was my inner calling, I could touch more lives more profoundly than the science job would, the job with which I did not feel a deep connection.

I had taken actions fearlessly many times before in my life, not because I was not aware of the challenges, but in spite of them. I strived for success despite the difficulties and I believed that this time it was achievable. I understood that courage is a great element of success, and I was willing to be courageous and stay true to myself at this important life junction. The career change I was contemplating was an occasion in which I felt called upon, and I could not suppress my feelings.

Before I made the decision to quit my job, I had already bought the tickets for a three-week visit to China in September 2013, with Amanda and Maureen.

My boss was kind enough to allow me to take a paid vacation right before my official last day of work, so my health insurance covered me while traveling. Even though I ended up not pursuing science, I was very grateful to my kind boss who was so supportive and understanding of my decisions.

Even though I left science as a career, I had great respect for the many scientists who are pushing forward to figure out and understand nature, the universe and ourselves. Many scientists place less importance on material belongings, but are truly passionate for the advancement of science and humanity and have dedicated their lives to scientific discoveries. Science and technology would not be where they are today without determined and talented scientists. It is about the meaning in your mind, your life's purpose, and the role you are destined to play in the greater good for humanity that makes a meaningful career for you. As for me I felt there was something else for me, and it was not a science career. When you are in alignment with your life's purpose you will feel called upon to do what you ought to do.

When I returned from China in October, my two and a half years of postdoctoral fellow work officially ended, and I felt a sense of relief. But at the same time, I was apprehensive about what the future held. I felt like I entered another tunnel that was the passage to my higher purpose. I was optimistic yet anxious to embark on this new adventure; I was ready for challenges that I knew were part of the journey.

Healing Others, Healing Myself

I set about increasing my knowledge of hypnosis and, in doing so, began to understand how the subconscious mind affects health, happiness, and success.

I obtained hypnosis certification before I quit my job and I started a practice towards the end of 2013, about a month after my trip from China. I rented a shared facility with a group of holistic practitioners, and went there twice a week, but I hadn't yet built a steady flow of clients.

Having spent all my life in science, I didn't have any business experience at all. I had no idea how to run a business or how to get clients. I decided to look for volunteers on Craigslist as a good place to start.

There was one fellow, among a few others, who came to me as a volunteer. He said that he had some psychological issues for which he was seeing a psychiatrist, and that he had been taking medication for years. It started when he was working in an extreme work environment a few years earlier. The job was so intolerable that one of his co-workers committed suicide and this had left a big impact on him psychologically. He started suffering from depression and nightmares. After he left that job, he couldn't work, as the experience was still troubling him. It was classic post-traumatic stress disorder.

As a hypnotist just starting out, I didn't expect a client to have such complicated issues, but luckily, I didn't place any predefined restraints on myself either. I gave it a try and induced hypnosis in him.

His face seemed so calm, peaceful, and serene as he entered hypnosis. I did the therapy work, and tried to release the fear embedded in his subconscious mind, and heal his inner self. I took him back to his younger self and re-instilled courage, confidence, and self-love. I had him repeat after me loving words about himself to instill self-confidence and the courage to move on. I helped him finish the unfinished business from the past and empowered him to move on with his life.

I saw the change in his face, and it was so profound. When I brought him out from hypnosis he was so refreshed. He was awed and said that he had never experienced anything like it before. I knew that it transformed me just as much it did him.

Afterwards, he emailed me about what a difference it had made in his life. Since our session together he never had the repeated nightmares again in the years that followed. It produced such changes that he felt he was looking at life completely differently, with a new set of eyes. It really surprised him, and as well as feeling proud of him, I felt new confidence in my ability to heal too.

Awakening to my own ability to make fundamental shifts in people's lives gave me great pleasure. This was something that I had been seeking for so long – the power to help people change their lives in a way they never thought possible. And it had come so naturally.

I had never found anything else so satisfying. The moment you can tell that someone has fundamentally changed and been "reborn" is the moment you find yourself being reborn too. I saw the power of my new skill, not only in healing others, but making me more complete in the process.

My husband was happy about my progress too, and the fact that I was doing something I was truly passionate about.

Life Finds a Way to Surprise Us All

Soon after I started hypnosis service, I missed my menstrual period that month. I had just returned from the three-week trip to China and I was going through a career change. I reckoned that perhaps I had been stressed looking for a place to conduct hypnosis and find clients, so I didn't take it too seriously. In addition, I had also had an IUD fitted since giving birth to Maureen, and was assured by my doctor that it was an effective birth control method.

David suggested taking a pregnancy test just to rule out the possibility that another baby was on the way. I didn't really think there was a need but it couldn't hurt.

To our huge surprise, it came back positive! At the time, Maureen was about a year-and-a-half and Amanda was a little over three; I had just quit my job and hadn't even started earning a steady income yet. We were definitely not ready for another child. My mind was racing, and I didn't know whether to laugh or cry.

David was in the living room relaxing on the computer while I was awaiting my result. I came downstairs with the test in my hand and I said, "You're not going to believe this…" He froze for a few seconds, speechless. I said: "Yes, we are pregnant!"

He was shocked, almost horrified. He even uttered the "F" word in despair! Neither of us could say a thing. We scheduled an OB appointment with the same doctor who had placed the IUD, and another pregnancy test confirmed the result.

The doctor reasoned that even though IUD is over 99% effective it is not 100%. We had to deal with what we got. We had two options: an abortion, which would be easy to do since it was so early in my pregnancy; or have the baby. Regardless, he would take out the IUD, but he warned that during the process there was a risk of the embryo detaching and causing a miscarriage. During our appointment, we saw the little "blob" attached to the uterine wall in the ultrasound. No doubt a new life had surely made its appearance.

After the appointment, David and I came home not knowing what to do. He argued that we weren't ready to have a third child. We already had two babies and our life was so hectic right now. Our financial situation definitely wouldn't allow it. I didn't have a career yet, and was still trying to establish myself as a hypnotist. Another baby wasn't an option. We should go for an abortion.

I thought differently. I felt a deep connection with this life that had been able to break through and survive an IUD. This being was deliberately seeking to be born and was finding a way! I was awed by the power of life. I felt that it was meant to be and that we should carry this life into the world. Somehow the maternal instinct kicked in and I felt the deep connection with this new life.

However, I couldn't convince David. He became stressed and insisted that I have an abortion. He listed all the reasons we should not have another child at this time. I became upset on hearing that and I would say, "OK, let's have the abortion," in an angry tone. But he knew I wasn't sincere about it.

For some hard to define reason, he soon came around and we decided to keep the baby. Maybe he was trying to please me, and not make me upset, or maybe I convinced him that we needed to bring this life into the world. Either way, my strategy worked.

The next big task was to inform his family that we were having yet another baby. This was problematic because my in-laws knew that we were under financial stress after I quit my job. But we had to break the news, no matter how shocked they might feel.

Ironically, my father-in-law had recently proposed to David that he should have a vasectomy. Even before our trip to China he was urging my husband to set a date and have it done. My husband agreed and said he would get it done, but clearly it wasn't soon enough.

My mom was living with us at the time, and we decided to arrange a family dinner at our house to break the news. Everyone had a great time and, after dinner, my father-in-law was happily chatting away, but he was concerned about me finding a job. David's aunt and grandma were there too, enjoying the time together. By the time they were ready to leave, we still hadn't plucked up the courage to break the big news. David was supposed to tell his family, but he just couldn't find the words. He kept pouring more wine, trying to summon up the courage.

Just as David was starting to make the announcement, my mom couldn't wait any longer, and jumped up and pointed to my belly, saying with her limited English, "Baby, baby!" They understood from my mom's body language and simple words, and they were shocked. My father-in-law was still chatting with someone in the living room and didn't hear what was going on. David's stepmom figured it out by my mom's expression and yelled out to David's father, "Sue's pregnant!"

My father-in-law turned his head and froze. His mouth and eyes remained wide open and he didn't move for a good five seconds. He looked like a statue. He struggled to come to terms with what was going on and lost his train of thought completely. It was an odd moment, and he didn't know whether to say "congratulations" or something else.

There was so much uncertainty. David's whole family was worried and didn't know if we would be able to handle the situation. But, after the initial shock, they all happily accepted the fact that we were going to have a third addition to our family.

When I was five months pregnant we found out that we were going to have a boy! David and his family were all thrilled that, after having two girls, we would now have a boy. My father-in-law was especially excited, thinking about all the boy toys he could buy and imagining the joys of spending time with his grandson.

Amid all the excitement my husband turned around and said, "See! You wanted an abortion! You're so terrible!" He was just joking, and I retaliated, "That was you!" David never runs out of energy to tease me and make jokes out of it. He is as mischievous as the first time I met him. Sometimes he distorts things to his favor and makes fun out it to make me laugh. He never runs out of ways to entertain me.

The Universe presents you with situations, but your choices and decisions are guided by your free will and inner voice. At any moment in life you are making choices, some may seem not critical, while others are life changing. The Universe presented to me a new life at a time when I least expected it. I believed that an abortion would be a betrayal of both my inner voice and the universal spirit permeating my life.

In fact, I was often amazed by how my third pregnancy occurred; it still feels unbelievable how this new life found its way when there seemed no chance. I was stunned by how strong the life force must be. I chose to believe that it was a gift from the Universe and I decided to carry this life to this world to fulfill its destiny. Isn't life powerful and awe-inspiring?

When you make life choices from your innermost feelings in line with the Universe you are doing the good deeds. Appreciating other people's lives, even if it's an unborn child, is a virtue that speaks out loud of who you are.

An Online Opportunity

We felt very blessed by our unexpected new addition. When I was about four months pregnant, I felt that it may not be convenient for me to do hypnosis while carrying a baby, so I stopped going into the office and started to look for a temporary alternative.

I was looking for something I could do online and improve my online marketing skills, as I believed that understanding business operations was an important part of growing my hypnosis business. I stumbled upon an opportunity that was advertised as a franchise model.

I was a little skeptical at first, but the video tutorials convinced me that it was going to work out because they showed many testimonials from everyday people making profits with this model. I had never encountered anything like this before, and I was curious about the bold promises. It would also take me step by step from a beginner to a marketing guru. I wanted to test it out, and therefore got into the program at $2,000. But I was soon told that I needed to invest another $9,000 to get the better benefits and earning potential.

The coach who helped me go through the training was an NLP (Neuro-Linguistic Programming) and sales expert. He built up rapport and trust with me; he gently guided me to the sales without any pushing. He assured me that with this advanced level I would be given help for personal branding that would make my business stand out; it would make a real difference.

I knew that with me being four months pregnant and that I was new to internet marketing I would need that kind of leverage. And that's where I made the mistake. My husband was against me investing in this company, but I persuaded him to lend me half of the money I needed. I got the other half from a friend of mine. That's when the nightmare started.

Soon after I wired the money at the end of 2013, the NLP and sales coach never responded to my messages again. And the company did not offer refunds! I was still able to communicate with many other members in the company, but the branding services were never offered. I was kicked to the curb and left alone.

As I reflect back, the thing that got me was that I was so naïve in the online world that I didn't know there were so many scams, even when the company presented itself professionally, and with countless seemingly convincing testimonials. On the other hand, I was shocked that such powerful skills as NLP not only can be used to heal and empower others, but can also trick and harm others when used by malicious-minded actors.

For a long time, I couldn't believe what had happened to me. The feeling of being a victim certainly welled up sometimes, and I felt resentment towards the internet marketing company and the coach who gave me empty promises. However, I soon had to let go of the negative feelings because I found myself using them as an excuse to earn sympathy instead of moving forward. I realized that I should not focus my energy on past mistakes. There was nothing more productive than using the experience as an important learning lesson. When everything is viewed as a learning lesson, there were no mistakes, only catalysts to become wiser.

My biggest mistake was that I let go of my personal power. I assumed that people would be considerate of my situation of being pregnant and starting a new career, and therefore they would help me with honesty. I assumed that some outside forces would help me, such as the internet marketing company or the coach. Had I remained in my own power I would have known that I was the only one who could help myself; I would not have surrendered my own power and let myself be taken advantage of.

I learned that at any moment in life always trust yourself and don't surrender your power to others. Not everyone with powerful skills, such as NLP and sales has the true intention to help others. When someone allegedly helps, ask yourself, do they intend to awaken your power within you or do they perceive themselves more powerful than you? Are you stepping into your own power or are you surrendering your power to others? Even if you make a mistake, what is the lesson to learn so you become stronger?

Marriage Taken to The Brink

After the internet scam, I decided to let it go, move on, and start from scratch to learn marketing skills. David helped me find some online training, as he wanted me to learn some real-world skills. I spent countless hours watching videos and practicing how to build a website, design graphics, and execute social media marketing, branding, copywriting, and even simple computer programming. My science background did help me in some ways because I was able to learn different knowledge and skillsets rather quickly, all while watching my two children and being pregnant with my third.

It was quite hard to balance it all, family and learning new skills. I seized every minute I could and worked late into the nights. I devoured training after training and many self-improvement books, and tried to keep myself in a positive vibe.

However, we didn't have much income, just my husband's job, and that wasn't enough to pay the monthly bills. David was becoming frustrated and impatient, and as I worked hard to learn the necessary skills for marketing, he unfortunately turned to alcohol and became increasingly distant.

He felt that I had not been considerate enough of our family, and this led to a lot of friction and fights over almost everything. The fact that I was spending all my time trying to master marketing skills didn't help, as I had been spending little time with him and sometimes totally ignored him. I felt that we were growing further and further apart to the point that I felt that we were moving on separate paths. It was unpleasant and uncomfortable sometimes to even see each other. Regardless of the reason of our quarrels it was always directed to me wasting money on an internet scam and not going to a 9-5 job. It always came down to David being mad at me irrespective of whatever we were trying to solve in the first place. It became a huge pain to communicate with each other.

I felt that we were impeding each other's progress. Perhaps we had different expectations of the other person. Perhaps our lives would be better without each other. Our fights intensified and led to three separate divorce crises.

One time I was working late into the night while he played video games all night and drank. He came into the bedroom and he said that he'd rather I work at a job, and be a mother again and a real wife. I sensed the fire in what he said, and threw back that I expected someone better than him. And he got very angry.

He said, "You're saying you want to leave me? Why not just leave? How many times do you need to threaten me?"

I was so mad hearing that, and wondered why I should stay with someone like him. He had no long-term vision, only goals of temporary comfort. He could not think or act in the face of any challenges. I felt like all he did was play video games and drink. I was very disappointed. On the other hand, I was a loser in his mind because I quit my science job and bought into an internet scam. Every time I reminded him that he needed to work on self-improvement and get better temper control in front of the kids, he belittled me. He blamed his bad temper on me as I put him through too much. I was blamed as the reason for all his miseries. He didn't appreciate me; he said things so hurtful and disrespectful and I really felt that it was the end of our marriage. We seemed to have lost respect for each other. I didn't think we could work it out as there didn't seem to be any possible future between us.

I knew that I had taken risks, but had been willing to do that to bring my family to a better place. However, to my husband I was just someone not being considerate of our family. I thought that I could never change him and knew that he could never change me either. Maybe we were better off apart. A divorce seemed the only way out.

The day after our big quarrel, I went and obtained divorce papers. It seemed sad, but perhaps that was how our marriage was meant to end.

Later that day, David apologized and said that he was drunk during the fight; that he hadn't meant to yell at me. Separating and divorcing was never his intention.

I knew that he came from a broken family and he hated it, and he was trying hard to build a better family of his own. Apart from our fights, he was trying his best to be a good dad and husband, even though he had a short temper. He was blunt and at times said things that hurt, but deep inside he did not mean to hurt my feelings. When the internet scam incident was not on his mind, he was an intimate husband and loving father. He lost control when worries crept in.

The reason that he was so upset with me was because what I did hurt his feelings, even though I did not intend to do so. It was a lot that I had put him through, and the fact that he was still willing to stay together told me how much he wanted to work it out. It was a misunderstanding resulting from each of us projecting our expectations on the other instead of truly accepting the other person. We viewed each other in comparison with our perceived notions and we did not stand in the other's shoes.

We each wanted the other person to be in a certain way that was not their real self. The discrepancy we saw between our expectations and the reality was the cause of our pains. We wanted the other person to change to what we would like them to be, but it was impossible. I felt that leaving him would not be a solution and will not do anyone any good, and that we should forgive each other and work on solving our marriage issues. However, we continued to have fights on and off, more than at any other time in our marriage.

One night our first floor flooded with water. It was not the first time we had had pipe issues. We kept hiring plumbers to fix them and no one had done a good job. After all the outlay, David saw water on the floor and he was so mad. The anger spread to me while I was trying to calm him down, and instead he yelled at me, blaming me for everything. He said that it was because of me that he was under so much stress; and it was because of me that he was drinking more than normal.

I stopped him and told him that I was so sad. I was leaning on the couch crying, unable to get over the fact that he kept trying to escape reality by using harmful means.

Suddenly it felt like he was just a stranger, not the person I had married. He explained that the reason he had become so insane was because I put him through too much. I understood how he felt even though I knew that he could have stayed positive to life's challenges.

I realized that everyone is different in their interpretation of reality and life's challenges. Yes, I could move on from mistakes, and breathe through challenges and I had done that multiple times in my life, but my husband grew up in a totally different background where he never needed to deal with challenges as I had had to in my early life. Therefore, our life situation to him was very stressful and hard for him to cope with, understandably so. On the other hand, since I was pregnant, he certainly did not want me to know that he was so stressed. So, he kept suppressing it until he exploded in anger toward me.

I had been ignoring my husband. I was putting all my effort into something I thought was important. I wanted a better future for my family but somehow, I was neglecting my family. He clearly felt isolated, that I wasn't spending any time with him anymore.

I realized that a man needs care, a man needs a woman's love and affection, and time together. And it was my fault that I was looking too far into the distance, that I was ignoring my husband's feelings. It was because I was a risk taker - and I wanted to give him and our family a better future. But I shouldn't have put our relationship on the back burner.

I understand that a woman can make or break a man. I started to readjust myself and allocated time for attending to my husband's needs. Despite our busy schedules, we set time to watch movies, go out to restaurants, and share house chores. I knew that he was very family oriented, and that he was a loving husband and father. He almost never misses a kids' play date. We went on play dates together, and went on errands together, got groceries, made lunches for our children, and read bedtime stories. David was nothing short of a great husband and father. He was an intimate guy and we would shower together in the mornings. He took good care of our family and made it possible for me to work on my business. He lived a simple life and video games were his passion and way of relaxation. I began to really appreciate him.

Despite our cultural and belief differences, we decided to look at our relationship with greater understanding. We decided to not lose sight of the big picture. The way we met and the way we had evolved in the process of building our beautiful family showed us that we belong together. By being together and being there for each other in good times and bad, we grew stronger. To find the connection again and remain in a loving relationship did not require earth-shattering efforts. It was the little things that strengthened the relationship. The challenges we had encountered in our journey led us to a deeper understanding and acceptance of each other.

Marriage is a bonding of two people, completely unrelated, with the intent of living a joined life. You might be rooted in totally different cultural backgrounds and family relationships, and therefore it takes courage to get together and fully embrace each other. It might take a lot of effort, even compromise to make a harmonious marriage. Life is a lot easier when the two are united.

Even though a husband and wife relationship is not blood-related, it does not mean it should be taken lightly. On the higher spiritual level, the souls of husband and wife might be intertwined in many lifetimes before. There might be a deeper meaning to the two coming together in this world. Remember: *there are no coincidences.*

Later I learned from my spirit guide that my husband's soul was the one who volunteered to become my husband in this lifetime as a challenge when my life was designed in the spirit world. We had little to no common lives from the past. I felt that since we are here on earth to make a couple in this lifetime, and perhaps we may not even come across each other again in future lives, isn't it a good reason to cherish each other even more and live this life in a successful marriage? It was what was meant to be, and we are here to learn from each other and help each other accomplish a meaningful life. We expand each other's horizons and motivate each other to new heights. By being together building a loving relationship despite the significant differences, there are important life lessons to be learned along the journey.

All marriages are unions of two souls working together and helping each other achieve their higher goals. It is an intimate relationship that ought to be cultivated and cherished. It might not be always smooth, but like other areas in life with challenges comes important lessons and room to improve and grow.

Giving Back What I Had

I was induced to labor three weeks earlier than my due date because our son had stopped growing inside my womb. My OB doctor concluded that he would grow better outside of me rather than inside.

On a day in early June 2014 I was induced to labor. Luckily, the labor was smooth, and Anthony was born a very healthy baby boy, despite being the smallest of our three babies. My husband joked that I had "diminishing returns."

David's family was very excited for our new precious arrival, especially my father-in-law, who couldn't wait for the male bonding time he'd have with my son.

I was very grateful to our son for accompanying me during one of the most difficult times of my life, as I was trying to establish my online marketing business. It was also at a time my husband and I went through relationship challenges and came out the other side stronger.

Most moms and dads try to give their children a better future. When you start a family, life as you know it changes. You may have to deal with financial stress to make ends meet, and seek out additional sources of income, but you don't have the freedom that non-parents do, as you need to attend to everyone's needs in the family.

Our children, Amanda, 5, Maureen, 3, and Anthony, 10 months in 2015.

But no matter what happens, always remain in your own power and make conscious decisions. Even if you make mistakes, which is unavoidable in life, look at it from a learning perspective and grow stronger from the experience. Cultivate harmonious relationships with your spouse and don't lose touch with your love. Stand in your partner's shoes and feel what they're feeling so you two can understand each other's true intent. Don't expect the other person to change as you wish, you can only change yourself. Remember that the core issue of your relationship may not be what it appears to be on the surface, such as financial, but a deeper trusting issue. Focus on the love that united you together in the first place; it's your source of strength.

Looking back, I'm glad that I was able to peep behind the curtain firsthand to understand what goes on in the lives of people who strive to create financial freedom for themselves and their family. I came to know many people from around the world who were working on building income streams through an online business. I made many meaningful relationships in this process. I also realized that this was exactly what I had needed to form the foundation of my business and how I would like to serve others with trust and honesty.

I was generous in sharing my knowledge in the online space, and I was good at some unique skills. I was grateful that I could explain complicated techniques in layman language and that people loved my teachings.

On a night in October 2014, four months after my son was born, my husband and I had a dinner date. On our way to the restaurant I received a Skype message from a new contact. He only asked me three questions: "Do you offer private coaching?"; "How much is it?"; and "Where to send the money?" That's how I got my first coaching client.

It wasn't long until I found out that this client was a quick learner and was quite smart. Unlike most people I saw on the internet who would wait for everything to be ready before taking action, which never happens, he took fast action and did not seem to have fear of failure like most people I knew. It only took me several months to fully realize his true potential.

He started an offline business because Hurricane Katrina stopped him from going to college. Through his hard work and honesty his business flourished through the years and he had been featured on multiple media outlets. However, his work was so demanding that he spent most waking hours at his work even though he hired quite a few workers. Then he started a family and wanted to start a business online to gain leverage, which was why he sought me out after learning about my stories. He was fearful of internet scams and exposure of personal identity. Through one of our casual chats, I learned that his offline business provided him more than a six-figure monthly income! I felt so humbled that he wanted my coaching. I was very proud of this young black man.

After my first coaching clients, I had clients coming from Singapore, Thailand, the UK, Canada, and the US. I cherished each experience and spared nothing to share my knowledge and skills.

David and I posing in a relative's garden, summer of 2017.

Finding The Path

It was empowering to learn about other people's stories, how they got where they were, and why they wanted to be where they wanted to go. I saw people from all walks of life seeking success, and oftentimes bearing misunderstandings from their spouses in regard to their endeavors.

I witnessed again and again that success is more mental than physical. How you think determines what type of actions you will take and hence, the results you will get. More often than not, I saw that what people needed for success was personal empowerment and the realization of their own power.

Reaching to Higher Purpose

As I was business coaching, I still could feel the callings for hypnosis work. During all these times, I had been learning new skills in hypnosis and providing sessions on the internet.

I recognized a commonality between healing and success in general, both of which require fundamental elevation from a person's current mental states through individual empowerment. When you realize your true inner powers, anything is possible. Past disempowering beliefs will be abandoned and replaced with beneficial beliefs that will guide you towards your goal, be it healing to optimal health, or achieving success in a business venture.

Changes need to be made in the subconscious, or even beyond, at the soul level. When you know who you are at the soul level you will be amazed by your personal identity and the sense of purpose in life, which is incredibly empowering.

I read many books about past lives, both in this lifetime and previous lifetimes, and how they affect our lives today. Steven Parkhill's book *Answer Cancer* opened up my mind to how perceptions as early as in the womb by an unborn child can impact his/her life in profound ways that's life-determining. In addition, I saw great truth in Michael

Newton's books *Journey of Souls* and *Destiny of Souls*. The extensive studies recounted in the books confirmed who we really are and why we are here living a life going through life's challenges, and it all resonated with me deeply. I was amazed by the depth of knowledge and studies that are available to us on our ultimate identity.

In early 2016, I decided to incorporate the power of the mind in my coaching. I helped a client tap into the super conscious mind and come up with congruent marketing messages. He was able to visualize the sales process and even read out the excellent sales copies perceived in his mind's eye. All those were done in trance. I was again amazed by the power of the mind.

Next, I facilitated him in a session to meet up with my spirit guide just to see if we could get anything. To my astonishment, once he was in trance during which I guided him to a garden scene, he saw an old Chinese man wearing a long robe. He described him as being in his 70s with little hair. My heart was beating fast as it seemed a moment of truth for me; it was like meeting my supervisor and I was anxious about his comments on me and my life.

I facilitated a series of questions for my spirit guide, sometimes I asked the client to relay my spirit guide's answers back to me or have my spirit guide talk through him with his permission. My spirit guide, who revealed himself as Dezhung Rinpoche, told me my life's purpose is to heal and empower others, and that I was to be known as the author of this book. The purpose of this book is to heal and empower, and it is part of my journey.

I was awed by what I found. I always felt that I needed to write a book one day about how I transformed my own life from a poor naïve Chinese village girl to an American scientist, mother of three, and then moved on to my true passion of healing and empowerment. I wanted to share what I had gone through, how I made the decisions, how I overcame obstacles, and even how I made mistakes and learned the lessons in life to get where I am today.

My life stories were not only important lessons for me, but they could also serve as lessons for you, dear reader, if you so choose. My intention with this book is for you to draw any lessons that may benefit you, and guide you to reflect upon your own life with its challenges and blessings, view them as important lessons to make you stronger. Thus, hopefully, you will see the purpose in life and realize your own power.

Even though in the distant past I did not see the big picture of my life and was not clear about my life's purpose, I was guided every step along the way by my spirit guide and the loving Universe. Knowing my true identity made me realize that my soul being had lived many lives before. I had indeed died and been born countless times. With each lifetime, I learned important lessons and progressed in development and understanding who I am. I assumed different roles in past lives. Some were easy, some were difficult, but each one was so perfectly designed.

I felt that I met myself. I felt I was awakened, and there was no other choice but to live with my full consciousness now. It was amazing to know who I am and why I am here.

You might have already awakened to your soul being, or you might be on the journey. Whichever is the case, simply remember that you are unbelievably amazing.

The fact that we embarked on a physical life in this lifetime is a sign that we were brave and we were trusted by the Universe to complete our missions. If you are going through life's challenges or think that your life is particularly hard sometimes, remind yourself that the Universe invested in you and loves you unconditionally; the Universe does not put you through life's challenges with no reason. The road twists and turns, but the destination is bright. So enjoy your journey. Remember that you are powerful, and you are meant to be great! You just need to wake up to your own power.

Surrender is Power

Since childhood I was curious about what life was. It was unexpected that I had the encounter with my spirit guide, a wise being who's guiding me on the other side. I felt that the door was open, and I finally saw what's behind the veil. I felt immense love and trust placed upon me. The challenges I had gone through were never in vain. The sense of purpose enveloped me.

There is indeed another world, the higher spiritual plane, beyond the physical world that we know of. When we live a human life, our sensory "filters" narrow our senses to the physical world, and unfortunately many people do not see things beyond the "looks." Sometimes we desire things to happen in certain ways, and people to act the way we like, and anything that does not fit into what we want we make ourselves stressed and unhappy. But what if you choose to interpret everything from a higher perspective? What if all you see is good and every challenge is a chance to grow? What if you take ownership of the power that is yours?

When we awaken to our higher truth, we come to understand how loved we are by the Universe and how powerful we truly are. We will be a lot more content with life's happenings because there is a profound meaning behind everything. We see perfection in everything. We would also cherish each and every relationship because it teaches us lessons and makes us a better person.

When I asked my spirit guide who is someone important to me in this lifetime that I should know of, I was expecting to hear about some gurus, mentors, or even business partners. However, he said it was my husband. In fact, the book title my spirit guide gave me and told me I was destined to be the author of was: *Me and My Husband, A Lifetime Journey*. I didn't quite understand it. Certainly, my husband was important to me, but I didn't perceive him as *that* important. My spirit guide perceived me marrying my husband as a big life challenge accomplished.

In the spirit world, souls are divided into groups to provide a structure and support for learning. Souls within the same group reincarnate together more frequently as family members. Souls from neighboring groups may also reincarnate together with you in the same lifetime as someone important in your life.

My husband's and my soul were in different soul groups that are far away from each other. We hardly had any interactions together in the past. We might have had one lifetime together hundreds of years ago in Denmark, where we reincarnated as neighbors with a cordial relationship. That's all we had in common in past lives.

When my life was designed in the spirit world, two souls volunteered to become my husband. One was my husband David, and the other one was Jian.

Jian and I shared two past lives both as husband and wife. My husband's volunteering to become my husband in this lifetime served as a challenge, and was agreed upon. We agreed to take the roles of husband and wife in this lifetime before reincarnation. That was the plan. Being able to marry my husband was a crucial point for the success of my current life.

However, while we live out the real life on earth we face the challenges of difficult choices. When I was trying to come to America, in the most difficult times of my life, I met Jian. Me meeting with Jian was a serious test from the Universe. It was a much easier path for me to choose Jian. Getting off the train at this station would mean I didn't need to struggle for something far-reaching in a painstaking endeavor. I would obtain personal comfort and ease, but I would not have the personal growth I was seeking. It was my alternative fate.

This alternative fate would mean I would have not much personal development. It was a test from the Universe to see if I was committed to my dream of coming to America to reach a bigger mission.

I had an inner knowing that with Jian it was the Universe testing my abilities. It was a feeling of surrender to the Universe and trusting that there was a plan for me, even though I didn't know what it was back then.

It was the Universe that planned things out so perfectly. Upon understanding what the plan was before reincarnation through the conversation with my spirit guide, I felt a sense of powerlessness. This powerlessness is not contradictory to the notion that we all have the free

Me and my family in Connecticut, summer of 2017.

will to choose and determine our own destiny. This powerlessness is the feeling of letting go and fully trusting the perfection of the Universe. This powerlessness is giving up resisting and letting the power of the Universe run through you. This powerlessness is the ultimate power.

    I am amazed by the perfect design of the Universe and I am immensely grateful for what I had gone through. It suddenly dawned upon me that there was never struggle or hardships; everything was perfect all along, and the Universe was with me every step along the journey. It was not me making the choices, but the Universe expressing through me. I myself was nobody; I was simply a conduit, a channel. Upon this realization tears swelled up. I was moved by the beauty of life and that I was powerless yet powerful.

    I'm greatly honored to have written this book to pass on this knowledge, once again with the Universe's help. With my free will I decided to change the title from *Me and My Husband, A Lifetime Journey* to *The Healing Journey* because I felt that this journey is about healing and understanding who we are and, therefore, making powerful choices in life. My spirit guide agreed.

I believe that everyone's life is a beautiful and perfect design by the Universe. When you want something, the whole Universe conspires to help you, as said in the best-selling book *The Alchemist*. You can live powerfully if you choose to let go and simply surrender. When you surrender, you are a channel for the power of the Universe to come through. There is nothing you cannot accomplish.

If you are embarking on a healing or empowerment journey through reading my life stories and the lessons learned, if you gained confidence to face life's challenges and difficulties, if you can move on with your life with great courage and self-love, there is no pride but only humbleness in my part; I am only a channel passing along the message.

Chapter 9

Lessons In The Higher Purpose

命运 *(Ming Yun) means destiny, fate, and what's meant to be. It may surprise you to know that, before your incarnation to this lifetime, you already agreed to it. In fact, you chose this lifetime, with all the challenges in it to foster your own development.*

An ancient Chinese poem goes:

"So it is that whenever Heaven invests a person with great responsibilities, it first tries his resolve, exhausts his muscles and bones, starves his body, leaves him destitute, and confounds his every endeavor. In this way, his patience and endurance are developed, and his weaknesses are overcome."

Could it be that the challenges you encounter in life are the exact things you need to make you stronger?

Sometimes life feels unbearable because of the challenges we come across. We feel helpless, frustrated, or might even feel life is not worth living when we are devastated. Why did you come across the challenges that you did? Is there a higher force at play for your life's happenings? What were the meanings behind? Could it be for your higher good?

I understand that these questions may not be the first ideas coming to your mind while you are undergoing pressure with serious life challenges. However, if you tap into your soul being and seek your higher purpose you will become grateful for them. There is no better way to foster your own development, if you open up to it, than those challenges you encounter. Therefore, it is not a coincidence that you come across the particular roadblocks. Indeed, your soul had deliberately chosen these challenges before your reincarnation. The difficulties you face are the exact elements to make you stronger. The Universe provides you with the opportunities to grow.

It may feel like a hard pill to swallow that you chose your life with its challenges before birth; you'd rather your life be smooth sailing without the storms. I know how you feel, because I have been through serious challenges, as you have seen in this book. We come to this world with a mission, which is our life's purpose. As we work toward fulfilling our life's purpose, we come across difficulties that challenge us and test our abilities, so that by the end of our life we will have progressed further as a being with the challenges we conquered under our belt. Challenges and difficulties are valuable lessons, if viewed from a higher perspective.

It is therefore no accident that you experience them. They are a test for you, they are a trust the Universe places upon you! It forces you to improve upon your existing abilities, instead of seeking personal comfort and settling for your lot. When you look at life from this angle, can you meet life's challenges with more confidence and gratitude? You should cherish them!

Life is a journey. It's not an easy journey, and there are going to be many challenges, roadblocks, and even sacrifices along the way. But how can you beat the odds in difficult situations and make better decisions and design your destiny?

The answer is in *how* you face the challenges coming your way. From this point on you decide to cope with tough situations with sure confidence in the face of life's challenges. You feel at ease to make better decisions in difficult times and no longer feel crushed or powerless. You awaken to your inner strength and find your true power, which is always within you.

Free Will

Even though our life challenges were chosen before we came to this lifetime, nothing is set in stone. The most powerful ability that we have is our free will. It means that we have the freedom of choice, and it is through this that we create our own destiny.

We all have the freedom to choose and make decisions in our lives. Every decision we make right now shapes our future in that direction, and it determines subsequent situations and further choices that we will face. As all the choices we make line up in the dimension of time, we are writing out our own destiny. Therefore, we are the co-creator of our own fate. So, keep in mind that you have full control of where your life goes at any point in your life. You are the designer of your own life. The moment you realize that you have *choice* is the most transformational moment.

When I look back at my life, when facing my childhood difficulties for instance, I could have chosen to overcome the challenges and grow stronger. Or I could have chosen to feel defeated and blame life for being harsh on me. The choices were totally up to me, but they would lead me to totally different life situations and opposite fates.

A criminal may blame his or her felony on a poor family and upbringing. However, someone who achieved great success may also attribute their success to their poor family background. Even children from the same family, with the same upbringing, can end up with day-and-night differences in their lives.

These differences lie in the exercising of free will, what they choose to believe, and how they choose to live their lives. You can choose how you want to feel, instead of "choosing" what seemed like a "default" the outside world seemed to have placed on you.

What you see and feel in your mind is true and will occur. What you think about manifests immediately in the higher spiritual plane, but takes longer in the physical plane, provided that you don't nullify your original thought by an opposing thought. By holding your thought with persistence and intensity you can achieve wonders.

You yourself are the director of your life, consciously or unconsciously.

Your Choices

So how can you enhance your free will and make sure that it results in good things and gets you to where you want to be? The key is in cultivating positive thinking so that you can interpret physical reality in a way that benefits you.

Many people don't understand the power of their choices. They are run by their emotions instead of thinking deliberately and beneficially. Many people don't even realize that how to interpret the outside world in your mind is totally up to you. It is a powerful *choice* that you can make. Understand that it's completely up to you how you want to interpret the meaning of life events, situations, or other people. It has little to do with the actual thing that happened but rather how you make sense of it with your own mind. It could be a training process for your mind to deliberately make positive choices until a healthy habit is formed.

An experience could be viewed as devastating or as a learning experience for you to grow stronger. You have the power of choice here. It is totally up to you. Which one would you rather choose?

Each of us is a three-in-one deal: body, mind, and soul. We might identify with our ego, or we may have fears such as the fear of failure, the fear of being poor, or the fear of death. That's because we identify with our body and mind, but not our souls.

Our soul is eternal and it incarnates in this lifetime to learn important lessons towards an understanding of its true self. Our soul is our driving force in life, seeking expression of self. It only knows love, not fear. It is our true being.

Understanding your true identity helps you better interpret the happenings in physical reality and realize the choices that you have. You will realize that the only limitation is self-imposed.

Tap into your soul, exercise your free will, appreciate your body, and you will navigate through this physical world with more confidence and power!

How to Get What You Want: Think with Intention, Feed with Emotion

As an incarnated human being, we are so in tune with the physical world that we lose sight of the larger part of ourselves, which is our vibrational energy being. *Our soul is energy.*

Matter is also energy, as stated in Einstein's famous matter and energy conversion formula $E=mC^2$. Matter consists of vibrational energies with physical appearances perceived by our physical senses.

But physical senses are only a small part of our greater consciousness. Our physical sensations help us perceive the physical world. The larger reality is that everything is energy and it is the origin of where everything springs. Creation starts in the subtle planes of energy, way beyond the physical plane. What you see in the physical plane is simply an effect, an end result not the source.

To get what you want, you need to feed positive energy into it, because this is how things are created in the energy world that we live in. For humans, our energy is in the form of emotions and feelings, and the way we tap into the energy is by thinking with intention.

So how do we generate the emotions and feelings that are advantageous for our personal development? To find the answer, you must look inside of you, not outside. Your emotions should not be swayed by what's happening outside of you but directed by your inner being through your free will. How would you feel if you already got what you want? That's the feeling you should cultivate.

To create, you have to think within, because you are the co-creator, and the beginning of your creation starts with thinking with intention. It is up to you how you want to translate events and people into feelings. And the emotions and feelings that you hold have a profound effect on your life. Your emotions, positive or negative, will draw the corresponding situations and experiences to your life. You constantly create your immediate future!

Laying False Blame

You may think that things are out of your control. You may blame society, parents, or anyone but yourself. In other words, you view yourself as a *victim*. You will seek out more events and individuals to back up the "fact" that you are a victim. This emotion will direct your life and draw upon more things that strengthen this negative feeling in you.

The "victim mentality" blocks you from taking responsibility for your own life, you forget your own free will, and you drift through life hopelessly.

Judgments have strong negative consequences. Often, people judge events, other people, or anything that blocks their way, and they attach negative feelings to them. This is the underlying cause of wars, conflicts, and even religions bashing each other. We want to make ourselves look superior and show that our opinion is right and others are wrong.

But to what end? What good does it do, other than feeding your selfish ego? Sometimes it's good to yield. We are not here to judge, we are here to create harmony and peace, not by force but by understanding each other and letting go.

Sometimes silence speaks louder than words. Put your judgment aside and try to cultivate feelings of contentment, gratitude, and true happiness. It is a choice that you can make.

The Positive Choice

Positive emotions are the result of positive thinking. Positive thinking is a choice, a way of life. It is a skill that can be developed by your willingness to do so. And once you developed this skill, you'll have a much more joyful life and get what you want. Good things will happen to you, if you are open to creating positive emotions. There is no failure when you think positively, only delay in results. Have faith and trust the Universe. The choice is yours.

You may think that there is nothing happening in your life to make you feel good. This means that you are looking in the wrong direction, because it is not in anything that's happening outside of you to make you feel happy. Rather it is a feeling inside of you that you have the ability to create. Happiness is a choice and it comes from within.

We may not be able to change the facts, but we can interpret the facts in a different light, more positively, and this will propel us to the next level of our development. We need to cultivate a higher understanding of reality and hold in our minds positive emotions and attitudes. If you don't know how to generate positive emotions, or if you are someone who only judges things by how they look, then use your imagination.

As Einstein said, "Imagination is more important than knowledge." Knowledge is facts and you can receive them passively by simply being told so or acquire it first-hand through your own experiences. It is about getting to know something that already exists. However, imagination is a mental ability to form an image that is not perceived by the physical senses, it is a creative process that allows you to bring something into existence. All the happenings, forms, or whatever we perceive with our physical senses were creations in the mind originally. Therefore, to get what you want, direct your emotions to a positive imagination of a desirable future. Make it real in your mind and fully experience it in your mind's eye and act in line with your deep thoughts. This way you will get what you want with least resistance.

Why is this true? It's because, as a soul, that's how we manifest things in the spirit world. By thinking of something we immediately bring it to reality. In the physical world, the time it takes to manifest is longer (therefore patience and persistence is required) but the principles are the same.

As human beings, we tend to use our left-brain to collect sensory information, analyze, judge, and criticize things. Many people have a hard time accepting anything without hardcore facts, reducing the role of imagination and intuition in their lives and just relying on facts and judgments. But when you imagine something, you send out energy to it. The more energy you put in the more you will draw upon the thing you imagined. Hold your desired outcome as a fact that's already happened; don't entertain any doubt or negative feelings.

The future contains the possibility of your desired outcome, as well as possibilities for failures and other undesirable outcomes; any of those possibilities could come true in reality. By focusing your energy on your desired outcome instead of failures, you feed energy into it. When you believe something with conviction, when you put faith in it without any doubt, when you block the possibility of failure, you cannot help but manifest your desired outcome. This has been tested time and time again. Your thoughts, intentions, imagination, feelings, and emotions have much farther-reaching consequences than you might have thought.

When you imagine that you are in a garden, you send thought forms of yourself there. Even though the happening is not physical, it happens in a higher dimension. The thought form as energy that you send out may not be visualized by physical eyes, but it can be detected with higher consciousness. Whatever you imagine, it is real in higher dimensions. The power of your thought is far more powerful and creative than you ever imagined. So think responsibly and deliberately.

Imagining Your Dream Future

The advancement of quantum physics provides insights into how we create our future. Quantum particles exhibit both features of particles and waves/possibilities, and whether or not you see a particle or waves/possibilities is dependent upon the behavior of your observation. In other words, the simple act of you observing, hence your consciousness, changes the nature of the event.

The future exists in the form of possibilities like the position of quantum particles, and the way to change/direct your future is by thinking in the moment of now of a particular possibility. When you think about a particular future outcome you are actually changing your future to that direction, just like your observation changes the behaviors of quantum particles.

The more you think about a particular future possibility, such as being healed or achieving business success, for example, and you feed it with positive emotions, the more that future ceases to be a mere possibility and becomes a reality. Your simple act of thinking makes the future become a fixed "particle."

Some people do this subconsciously in their lives and they appear to be lucky to you. But you can become lucky too! Good things happening to you is a possibility, so why not make that possibility 100 percent? Good things can happen to you if your mind is open.

Think with intention, and feed it with emotions. Then you can get what you want in life.

Who Are You?

You are more than who you think you are. Your name does not tell you who you are, it's just a label. Your parents and birthplace do not tell who you are, they just tell you how and where you came into this world. Your hair color and skin do not tell who you are, they just show how you look. Who are you really? And why do you think you were born into this world? Where are you going after death?

We are spiritual beings, incarnated in physical forms to accomplish our goals towards understanding our true identity as beings, and to improve our abilities. We are here to learn how to love each other and understand our relationship with the Oneness. When you love others like you do yourself, when you help others like you help yourself, you've achieved a higher understanding of the true nature of life. When you give other people as much credit as you do yourself, it means that you understand that we are all created equally, that we are separate but interrelated entities from the same Oneness.

Compassion is a quality that measures your spiritual advancement. Other souls sensing through other bodies, meaning other individuals, share the same type of sensations, feelings, and emotions that you do. They feel sadness or happiness, pain or pleasure, hate or love, and any other feelings, just like you do. You see separateness because you cannot directly perceive from another person's consciousness, but in a sense, other individuals are you and you are other individuals. You and I are no different than he or she. We are all the same.

However, each of us is also unique. There's never a second you throughout history across the globe. Each of us is unique so that we can experience life from different perspectives. We are part of the collective consciousness, the Oneness, but we often lose sight of it while facing life's challenges. We forget our true identity and live by a narrow sense of self.

Each of our individual souls incarnate throughout history in different bodies with different races in different eras in different countries filled with different stories while carrying out our different missions. Through living a physical life throughout time and space in all walks of life, the ONE consciousness gains learnings through different perspectives through each of us. We are all channels for the same source. The same source is expressing itself through every single one of us. We are like different leaves on the same tree, we are the same yet each unique in its own way.

The advancement of humanity and progression of the higher spiritual plane depend on each of us. Love one another is our true nature.

My First "Out-of-Body" Experience

Many people have had an out-of-body experience and found it life changing, because it is a first-hand experience of your higher reality and shows that you are much more than your physical body. It elevates your consciousness and enables you to see the larger picture.

People who have had near-death experiences have reported out-of-body experiences where they detached from their physical bodies, saw the divine light, or met their loved ones on the other side. They could see, even if they were physically blind, and were fully conscious in their out-of-body state.

This experience is transformational for many people, because they are awakened to the fact that death is not the end, and that there is life after death. They witness their true identity as an immortal soul being. After realizing this profound message, people's lives are transformed; they viewed life with expanded wisdom and ease.

The consciousness never dies. Upon physical death, it enters the higher spirit plane. Death is a time when you awaken. You will realize that living a physical life is your real "dream state" while being a spirit is your true nature and ultimate reality.

Upon returning to the spirit world you will recover your soul's memory of all your past lives and the lessons you learned as an intelligent being. You will study your past lives and explore alternative possibilities, and you can relive any past life and explore how it would feel if you had made better choices as a way to furthering your understanding of free will and personal improvement. You will use telepathy to communicate with other soul beings and help each other deepen the understanding of life. The afterlife is our heaven, while life on earth is more like hell.

Our biggest fear, the fear of death, is an illusion after all. There is nothing to worry about. Death is a new beginning. When humanity has risen to the level of perceiving death from a new positive perspective, we can truly consider ourselves "advanced."

Out-of-body experiences can also occur during astral projection or in our dreams while sleeping. However, you may not even realize it when it happens because consciousness may block the memory of it from the dream.

I had long been curious about the meaning of life as a young Chinese girl living on our farm. It was beyond my comprehension at the time and I never knew that I could get an answer myself one day. Fortunately, I had a brief out-of-body experience where I was conscious for part of the soul travel and it opened up my mind to a whole new level. Nothing compares to the profound experience of your soul being, even just the brief moments of feeling the soul coming out from the body.

One night while I was putting my two-year-old son to sleep I was drifting off to sleep as well. My body was so tired and in sleep, but my mind was crystal clear, and I was fully aware of my surroundings. I could feel my body in contact with the bed and I could feel each breath coming in and out. I felt that me and my body were two different things. Then I heard a roaring sound in my ears and felt a pulling sensation; I felt my soul slipping out from my crown chakra, at the top of my head.

I was a little startled and nervous, as I knew that my soul had traveled out of my body. I was still alert, but my body was sound asleep. All I could hear was the roaring sound like wind buzzing in my ears, but I knew something must be happening to my soul. After what seemed to be a few minutes, I felt my soul slipping back into my body through the crown chakra. I felt the merging sensation with my body. As soon as the merging was complete I woke up immediately, feeling a bit numb in my arms and legs.

Nothing is as convincing as something you experience firsthand. I was awed by the experience. Even though my consciousness was not able to travel with my soul, it was mind-blowing to have felt my soul leave the body to start the travel and then merge back with the body. Throughout the whole experience my mind was crystal clear and fully alert, yet I could also feel my body sleeping and breathing. I felt firsthand I was something more than my physical body. I had a glimpse of what "I" am.

After you experience your soul being, even just glimpses of it, things are never the same again. The ego starts to dissolve its restrictions as the consciousness broadens and becomes more accepting of the higher truth.

The more you identify with your soul being, the more you open up your mind. The more you open up your mind, the larger your consciousness expands, and the more harmonious and calm you will be in life.

Later, I facilitated a channeling session of my soul and asked about this experience. My soul said that she did leave at that time. I asked her where she went and she said that she went to the higher spiritual plane to learn how to benefit both worlds, the higher spiritual world and the physical world. I further questioned how could my consciousness perceive the trainings in the higher spiritual plane. She told me to focus on it when it happens.

The part of me who I think I am (the ego) and my true self (the soul) felt like two different entities, but I know that as my consciousness keeps expanding, the two will merge. When that happens, I will be enlightened with heightened consciousness that is limitless.

You might have experienced something like this already, but simply brushed it off as a dream. Or perhaps you have never thought about who you really are beyond the physical terms. But you can choose to begin living more consciously now and open up your mind to possibilities instead of restricting your mind to what was thought possible by others.

It requires discipline and concentration to retrain your mind, but awakening to your soul being and realizing your enormous power is well worth your effort. Your soul harbors great wisdom and has best interest in you, because it is the real you.

You don't have to wait until death to wake up to your true identity. What if you decide to awaken right now and use your soul's ability to benefit your life and that of people around you in this lifetime? What if you could experience eternity and make better decisions in life now? How will it feel if you can see the higher truth and approach life's happenings with calm and ease? Can you imagine yourself being happy regardless of the situation you are in? How would you feel and act had you known that you are loved *unconditionally*? What if you could understand relationships in a new dimension and approach people with true love and compassion? It starts with your decision to wake up and open up your mind to this idea.

The Perfection of Your Journey

As you go through life you will encounter many challenges, some of which may take you off track, make you feel frustrated, or even make you depressed. When you start feeling like a victim, step inwards so that you can start to see the whole picture of why it's happening. Stay true to yourself and remain centered.

The world you see is a perfect reflection of what you hold inside of you. You are exactly where you want to be in life, no more and no less. Your situations are the creation of your own mind and life decisions, consciously or unconsciously. And because your life happenings are results of your choice, you have the power to start choosing consciously and more powerfully and therefore, transform your life.

At any given moment in life you have the choice of how you want to feel. It is up to you how you choose to interpret the events and people in your life. What you choose in the moment of now determines your next set of new situations, which create further choices. The choices you make in life become your destiny. You have the free will to choose, so choose wisely and create your beautiful destiny!

Life is not a compilation of random events just to make your life harder or miserable. You have much more power and wisdom than you think you do; you are not a victim but a designer of your own life. The way you tap into that innate power within you is by getting in touch with your soul and understanding your life's purpose.

You are born into this world with a reason, and the challenges you face are the exact lessons you set out to learn. Ask the deepest part of you what your life is about and how the challenges you face help you grow as a being. You will know that there is nothing to resist, suffer, or fight against. Your journey is perfect, and you just need to truly accept it. You will see the perfection and beauty of your life design. It will then help you make better choices with expanded consciousness and higher understanding. You become happy, content, and harmonious from the inside.

You are on a journey to heal yourself.

About the Author

Sue Maisano is a Chinese American author and healer. She uses the power of the mind to help clients heal emotionally and create harmonious relationships where letting go is possible. Clients may experience healing of emotions, improvement of relationships, and balance in physical bodies. Her philosophy is reprogramming the subconscious and revealing the superconscious mind in order for clients to experience first-hand their expanded consciousness where healing and removing of the cause can happen. Sue has the gift of creating soul-deep self-discoveries in clients, by drawing from their deeper minds to elicit true understanding, forgiveness, acceptance and therefore real change.

Sue obtained her Bachelor of Science degree in Life Science from Beijing Normal University, and her PhD in Biology from Wesleyan University.

Sue holds certifications in the following areas:

- Hypnosis
- Reiki Master
- Silva ESP

In addition, she has studied extensively without certification:

- Life Between Lives Hypnotherapy by Michael Newton, author of *Destiny of Souls*
- Healing the Body Using the Mind by Steven Parkhill, author of *Answer Cancer*

Contact information:

Email: Sue@SueMaisano.com
Service Website: SueMaisano.com
Blog: www.MindRealities.com

www.ingramcontent.com/pod-product-compliance
Lightning Source LLC
Chambersburg PA
CBHW021146080526
44588CB00008B/240